303 Tween-Approved Exercises and Active Games

SmartFun Activity Books from Hunter House

303
Tween-Approved
Exercises
and
Active Games

AGES 9–12

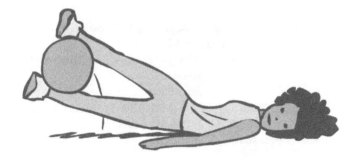

Kimberly Wechsler

Foreword by Leisa Hart
Illustrated by Michael Sleva

A Hunter House Smart Fun **Book**

Hunter House Inc., Publishers
PO Box 2914
Alameda CA 94501-0914

Library of Congress Cataloging-in-Publication Data
Wechsler, Kimberly.
303 tween-approved exercises and active games : ages 9–12 / Kimberly Wechsler.
p.   cm.
Includes index.
ISBN 978-0-89793-620-0 (pbk.) — ISBN 978-0-89793-625-5 (spiral)
ISBN 978-0-89793-633-0 (ebook)
1. Exercise for youth.   2. Physical fitness for youth.   I. Title.
GV443.W38 2012
613.7'043 — dc23   2012030704

Project Credits

Cover Design: Jinni Fontana	Rights Coordinator: Candace Groskreutz
Book Production: John McKercher	Publisher's Assistant: Bronwyn Emery
Illustrator: Michael Sleva	Administrative Assistant: Kimberly Kim
Developmental and Copy Editor: Amy Bauman	Customer Service Manager: Christina Sverdrup
Managing Editor: Alexandra Mummery	Order Fulfillment: Washul Lakdhon
Editorial Assistant: Tu-Anh Dang-Tran	Administrator: Theresa Nelson
Special Sales Manager: Judy Hardin	Computer Support: Peter Eichelberger
Publicity Coordinator: Martha Scarpati	Publisher: Kiran S. Rana

Printed and bound by Bang Printing, Brainerd, Minnesota
Manufactured in the United States of America

9 8 7 6 5 4 3 2 1   First Edition   13 14 15 16 17

Contents

Introduction: The Secrets of a Tween

The Exercises and Games

*A detailed list of the games indicating
appropriate group sizes begins on the next page.*

*Please note that the illustrations in this book are all outline drawings.
The fact that the pages are white does not imply that the people all have
white skin. This book is for people of all races and ethnic identities.*

List of Games

Upper Body

Get Your Game On!

High-Fun Warning

> *Most of the activities may be performed with groups of any size. A few are designed for pairs, small groups, or the whole group. These exceptions are individually marked with a group-size icon.*

Foreword

My three little blessings, Abe, eleven; Sam, nine; and Mary Frances, six, are daily reminders of how precious life is and how my husband, Jim, and I have the honor of guiding and nurturing them every single day.

More than anything, I want them to grow up happy, healthy, and with confidence to tackle life's challenges. I want to instill in them self-respect and give them the best possible chance for an enlightening education and a promising career path with tools to help them appreciate the gifts they are given.

As a yoga and fitness specialist, I am able to share my passion for health and wellness not only with my clients but also, first and foremost, with my family. My job as "Mom" is my most important role. My children are counting on me every single day, and I deliver as best I can by setting a good example of a healthy lifestyle in mind, body, and spirit.

Let this lighthearted book be your road map on your journey to guide your children along a path that will inspire them to embrace fitness for a lifetime. Taking simple steps will yield great results and have a powerful impact on the children in your life. I encourage you to have fun with the games and let your inner child come out!

Leisa Hart

Leisa Hart has worked in the fitness industry for over twenty-nine years and is best known for starring in eighteen of the popular Buns of Steel *exercise videos, which have sold over six million copies. She is the owner of Hart Yoga Pilates & Spa in Frisco, Texas. www.HartYogaPilates.com.*

Acknowledgments

I dedicate this book to all parents, caregivers, educators, teachers, coaches, volunteers, fitness instructors, athletes, day-care providers, camp counselors, and all others who know the importance of teaching and leading by example in promoting good health and ensuring that exercise becomes a regular and enjoyable part of daily life for children. These people know that exercise allows children to achieve their full potential and grow to be healthy adults. I dedicate this book to my husband, Jonathan; my children, Andrew, Addison, Courtney, Kyle; and to the rest of my family who are always there to support this food-loving, wellness-craving mom, wife, and daughter.

My website is www.FitAmericanFamilies.com.

Important Note

Introduction: The Secrets of a Tween

Part of the magic of tweenhood is the discovery of tweens trying to identify who they are and who they want to be; they are no longer children and not yet teenagers. Life tends to look black and white to them, so, at this stage, it is important to set guidelines of healthy living and exercise that will carry them on through their teenage and adult lives.

A Message to Parents and Other Caring Adults

This book, *303 Tween-Approved Games,* can be used effectively with or without the assistance of parents, teachers, or counselors. It is written for kids to understand the importance of living an active lifestyle. For adults, after you have read this book, set a fitness game plan with the kids, help set up the exercises for them, or better yet exercise with them.

Partnering with Your Pediatrician

The first step to take when making any changes in a child's current lifestyle is to partner with a pediatrician. You (or the parents of your students) should consult with the child's pediatrician to have a complete medical history, understand the child's body mass index (BMI), and to discuss any medical concerns, weight issues, unhealthy habits, or any other concerns you may have regarding your child.

If the child is obese or overweight, exercise alone will not help him lose weight, but a healthy eating plan with the right amount of calories will set him on the right path. This book provides over three hundred different exercises, physical activities, and sport drills to keep your tween physically active. A child with a chronic health condition or disability should not be excluded from physical activities; some of the exercises in this book may need to be modified to fit the needs of your child.

Kids between the ages of nine and twelve are considered to be in the tween or adolescent years. As mentioned above, these are the years during which they are no longer considered a child and yet they are not old enough to be considered a teenager. Kids of this age group begin to change in many ways— physical (including hormonal) and mental—that can have a huge impact on their beliefs, habits, attitudes, and lifestyles from now all the way through their adulthood. During this phase of childhood, tweens learn to become more independent. They form their own moral code, speak their opinions, pull away from parents, and begin to find a group of kids with whom they wish to identify. This is the beginning of developing who they are and what each of them as a person represents. Puberty begins at different rates during this period, making some kids bigger and stronger than others. You may find children of this age moody, short tempered, or rude. Anxiety begins to develop for some kids; they begin to feel stress from school, friends, family, sports, homework, and many other outside pressures. Body image can become an issue for some tweens; they become concerned with their clothes and how their bodies look. To keep tweens on the right path, it is important for parents, teachers, and counselors to communicate often with kids of this age, provide them with knowledge of a healthy and active lifestyle, lead by example, have a positive attitude toward healthy living, and communicate by being honest and direct. Also, show them you are listening and willing to respect the difference of opinions. Using verbal and nonverbal skills, show them you love and respect them always and teach tweens balance, moderation, and discipline in every aspect of their lives. Keeping kids on the right path to making healthy food choices and staying active is one of the greatest gifts you can give them.

What Can Parents and Caring Adults Do?

Kids at this age are very good at tuning out their parents, so, if you can, be clever and sneak in the occasional comment to reinforce the message that their sports activities and exercising games aren't just for fun but are also keeping them healthy. Kids at this age are very smart; they understand that it is unhealthy to sit all day watching television and eating junk food. But it is important that they understand the short- and long-term benefits of being physically active, too.

Here are some of the benefits of being physically active that you can discuss with your tween. Being physically fit will:

- increase energy expenditure
- help strengthen muscles and bones
- improve cardiovascular endurance
- burn calories
- improve self-esteem
- decrease risk of serious illnesses later in life
- help increase creative development
- teach problem-solving skills
- aid in motor-skill development
- bring family involvement
- improve coordination skills

- assist in social development
- teach sportsmanship
- teach them how to follow basic rules
- teach them how to receive direction from someone outside the family
- develop confidence
- develop cognitive thinking
- teach them about taking care of their bodies
- help them become more aware of their bodies
- help them sleep well
- give them a better appetite
- teach them to become more focused
- help them establish friendships
- aid in their developmental growth

How Much Exercise Does a Nine- to Twelve-Year-Old Need Each Day?

According to the American Academy of Pediatrics, children ages nine to twelve should be involved in heart-pumping activities, (cardiovascular or aerobic activity) for at least 60 minutes per day. This does not have to be continual play; it can be broken down into increments throughout the day and include 15 to 30 minutes of muscular resistance each day, which can add up to 60 minutes. Breathing fresh air is good for people, too, so 30 minutes of outdoor play is also highly recommended.

Guidelines of Exercise for Tweens

To fully benefit from an active lifestyle, it is essential not only to be active but to commit to a regular practice routine. It is important then to make sure tweens get enough rest, eat a healthy diet, find productive ways to reduce the stress that enters their lives, and keep a positive outlook on life. The tween body is not yet done developing, so we don't push a lot of weight training. In fact, this book offers a few exercises with light weights only—no heavy weights. Weight training is important, but overdoing the weight on a body that is not through developing can damage muscles and stunt growth plates. Use weights in low amounts (under 10 pounds), increasing resistance slowly as development and strength increase. Bands and tubes are recommended for strength training with tweens.

The most important key to an exercise plan for tweens is the cardiovascular component…and letting them choose the exercises they like best. It is so important to keep the heart pumping by running, walking, swimming, playing tag, shooting baskets, kicking a soccer ball, practicing martial arts/aerobic dance/circuit training, and performing skills and drills of a favorite sport. This book includes hundreds of movements to keep your tween's heart beating strong!

It is quite common for kids of this age to resist an exercise program if they are not currently active. You must be the catalyst to get the kids off the sofa and into an exercise program. Leading by example is the best way to start exercising, so why not develop a fitness plan together? The following are some suggestions for getting started.

Find the Right Type of Activity for Your Tween

Exercise is fun; you just have to find the right activity for your tween. There is the perfect exercise out there for them, but you must take into account individual preferences and personalities. Some young people thrive on competition; if that's true of the kids in your life, sports teams may be a good choice for them. Others have an aversion to highly competitive sports and may be far more motivated to try personally challenging activities such as hiking, swimming, bowling, yoga, and biking. Suggest activities that tweens will feel are within their current range of competence and skill level and to their liking. One major factor predicting whether your kids will become involved in a specific physical activity is the extent to which they believe that they have the potential to succeed and whether that activity is fun. Suggesting activities that tweens will feel are within their range of competence is especially important for those with limited experience in athletics or with obstacles such as obesity. And since kids at this age still enjoy doing activities with the adults in their lives, you can plan outings that involve physical activities. This will also create opportunities for you to spend quality time with the kids while having fun in the community.

Activities in Your Community

- batting practice
- biking
- bowling
- canoeing
- cheerleading

- fishing
- four-wheeling
- geocaching (see page 132)
- golfing
- hiking
- horseback riding
- jogging
- kayaking
- martial arts
- miniature golfing
- mountain climbing
- playing paint ball
- rock climbing (on indoor climbing walls)
- running obstacle courses
- skateboarding
- skiing
- swimming
- picking your own apples or strawberries at a local farm
- team sports such as baseball, basketball, tennis, archery, and badminton
- white-water rafting

Some Activities a Little Closer to Home
- cleaning out the garage
- engaging in an outdoor relay race
- having a water balloon fight
- helping with yard work
- holding a car wash
- participating in a family fun run
- playing a game of tag

Take Baby Steps

An hour of exercise a day can seem like a lot for anyone. If your tween is not physically active or is self-conscious about her body, it may feel overwhelming.

That's where you, the adult, come in. You can help the tween get moving and even work up to 60 minutes of exercise a day. Kids who aren't used to exercising may be willing to tolerate only a little physical activity before wanting to quit, so the belief that fitness means going from a sedentary lifestyle to running 5 miles every day makes the task overwhelming and totally unrealistic. Increasing daily physical activity by only 10 minutes a week makes it manageable.

The key is to start off small and provide plenty of role modeling and support along the way. Don't change a kid's lifestyle drastically in the beginning; rather, build on what the kid normally does during their day but encourage goals such as taking a walk or playing a game of basketball after dinner. Even making small changes—the goal of an extra half hour of exercise each day can be reached in just six weeks—can lead to a major improvement in fitness. For the first week, start with a total of 10 minutes three times a week. If a kid gets involved in the activities in the book, often he will go longer. If a kid thinks that he is going to practice just three of the sport drills in the book, he is much more likely to get off the sofa and exercise each time. When the task is broken down into smaller increments, the goal doesn't seem so big.

After the first week of exercising, the tween should be ready to increase the intensity of each exercise or activity; in other words, run a little faster or jump a little higher. Again, the key to sticking with exercise is doing things you enjoy. Aim for four days per week of moderate-to-intense exercise. Then start to incorporate some light resistance training into your routine. Change it up: Each week, try a new exercise or learn a new sport. From this point on, see if you can increase your exercise time by 5 minutes each week. Eventually your tween will be exercising for 30 to 40 minutes three or four times a week. Then start looking for creative ways you can sneak in more fitness each day; for example, suggest the kids take the stairs instead of the elevator or walk to school or to a friend's house. Remember, our goal as parents, teachers, and counselors is to create an active lifestyle for our kids.

Tweens Still Need and Want Your Approval

You may not believe this, but parents are still the central figure in their tweens lives no matter how hard a child tries to prove otherwise. It's just that tweens are trying to establish their independence, assert their desires to try new experiences, and practice making choices of their own. Even so, adult opinion and approval still make a huge difference in their lives; they just don't want you to know it. Show support, cheer them on whenever possible, attend their soccer games, and spend active time with them on weekends. Guide them, love them, and support them in their efforts every day.

Set small fitness goals with your kids. Be sure to set up a reward system when they meet a fitness goal. Little successes will also build your tweens self-confidence that he can make exercise a part of his life. Praise and encourage him for any positive steps he takes toward being healthier.

Home Environment

The habits that are developed in childhood often stay with a person through-out life, so exercise and active play need to be at the top of our priority list of what we want to model for our children. If you make a point of showing your tweens what an active, healthy lifestyle looks like, they are more likely to have a healthy lifestyle. So live by example; the less you say, the more you do will have an impact on your child. Getting the entire family involved and treating exercise as just another fun activity is one way to get everyone moving without applying too much pressure to participate in a rigid exercise routine.

For the best results, create the right environment—one that motivates kids to exercise and makes exercising enjoyable. Designate a space within your home that has enough room for exercising. Hang some inspirational posters or pictures of sport celebrities to inspire your kids. Consider having basic equipment available at home. For this age group, big, expensive pieces of equipment are not needed, but below is a list of recommended equipment for families to use for the exercises in this book.

Recommended Fitness Equipment for Tweens

- basketball hoop
- cones
- free weights
- golf clubs
- a pitching net
- tennis racquets
- tubes
- yoga mats
- broomsticks
- fitness balls
- goals
- jump ropes
- specific sports equipment
- towels
- a variety of balls

Get Active; Get Fit

It's very important to start young children with the right attitude toward exercise. Don't make exercise a chore and never use exercise as a punishment. Being physically active must be fun, or kids will have a negative attitude toward it. Not all kids are natural athletes, and, unfortunately, some kids believe that they can't be active. But that thought couldn't be farther from the truth. Today, we have hundreds of different styles of exercises, sport drills, and active games to keep kids moving. The most important aspect of getting kids to exercise is to make sure they're having fun, so you should work with your tween's personality and fitness level in finding enjoyable fitness activities.

Tweens get less than 15 minutes of vigorous physical activity a day.

Kids in this age group tend to like sports including (but not limited to): aerobics, archery, badminton, baseball, basketball, bicycling, billiards, bocce ball, bowling, boxing, canoeing, cheerleading, circuit training, cricket, cross-country skiing, curling, dancing, darts, diving, downhill skiing, fencing, fishing, football, ultimate frisbee, geocaching, golf, gymnastics, handball, hiking, hockey, horseback riding, hunting, inline skating, juggling, kayaking, lacrosse, martial arts, mountain biking, mountain climbing, orienteering, paddleball, Pilates, polo, racquetball, roller skating, rowing, rugby, running, sailing, skateboarding, skating, skiing, sledding, snorkeling, snowshoeing, soccer, softball, squash, surfing, swimming, table tennis, tai chi, tennis, track and field, volleyball, walking, water skiing, weight training (light weights only), white-water rafting, and wrestling.

Unfortunately, kids in this age group have the highest dropout rate when it comes to organized sports. Therefore it is vital to their health to find alternatives to keep them active. Set up an exercise program using this book, join a gym, work out as a family, play tennis, shoot some hoops, kick around a soccer ball, go hiking or mountain climbing. Just go outside and let the world be your gym.

My daughter has a negative attitude toward exercise.

Even household chores are a physical activity, and they can teach tweens responsibility and respect for their family and their surroundings. Within this age group, kids can do almost any chores. Assign them to clean their bedrooms. Don't let them stop at just making the bed, but, rather, have them tackle everything that is involved with keeping their rooms clean. Or see what other household chores they can handle, such as vacuuming and sweeping floors, dusting ceiling fans and furniture, doing their own laundry, putting away clean clothes, cleaning their bathrooms, making lunches, cleaning dishes, making dinner, taking out the garbage. Think of this as a training period for adulthood. And always give plenty of praise when a job is done—let them know contributing to a family is a good feeling.

Even just setting house rules can give tweens direction. Limit "screen" time, phone time, and sitting time, and encourage more active play. The American Academy of Pediatrics recommends no more than two hours a day of watching TV or playing video or computer games. So work together with your tween to set house rules on screen time.

My ten-year-old prefers to spend his time in front of the computer and television.

The more time you spend in front of the television or playing video games, the less time you have to be active. Not being active is a major contributing factor to an unhealthy body. Leading a sedentary lifestyle can cause weight gain and even obesity, which can lead to high blood pressure, high cholesterol, type 2 diabetes, and other diseases of the body. You don't have to be an athlete or be involved in an organized sport to be fit, you just have to sit less and move more. There are over three hundred different exercises in this book; read through and find the right ones for your tween.

Safety Comes First

We want our children to have healthy bodies as they explore their new active lifestyles, so to prevent them from any injuries, it is important that they use the right safety equipment. For instance, helmets are needed for sports such as baseball, football, softball, biking, snow sports, and rollerblading. It is important that your tweens wear the right helmet for the sport that they are playing. The helmet should have a sticker from the Consumer Product Safety Commission (CPSC), which means that it is safe for a particular activity, such as biking.

Other safety pieces include mouth guards, body pads, and eye gear. If children are playing any activity in which there is a chance of getting hit in the head, or specifically the face, they need to get a mouth guard. You can get mouth guards from a dentist or a sporting goods store. Elbow, knee, and wrist pads should be worn when skateboarding, snowboarding, skating, or playing ice hockey to help protect against broken bones. And special eye protection is needed for sports such as ice hockey, lacrosse, and racquetball. Make sure the goggles and face masks fit snugly against the face.

Training Principles for All Exercises

In order to get the most out of training, you must follow these simple principles.

Teach Technique

It is important to teach children the proper technique in any type of exercise, sport, or movement. Read each exercise description fully both to yourself and to the kids, and be sure to carefully observe and guide the child's movement. Focus on the technique and not on the resistance of the movement.

Consider Range of Motion

For full development of a muscle group, exercise through the range of motion, all the way up and all the way down.

Control Speed of Motion

Execute each movement slowly to avoid injury and to ensure the exercise is done correctly. The more control children have of each movement, the more improvement they will see.

Include All Aspects of Fitness

This book contains all aspects of fitness: stretching and flexibility, strength training for endurance and power, cardiovascular endurance, balance, visual tracking, gross motor skills, and meditation.

Listen to Your Body

As you perform the exercises, pay attention to how your body is reacting. Do you feel pain or stiffness in any area of the body? If so, stop the exercise, read the description again, and try the exercise one more time. Try exercising every day, even if it is a light workout.

The Intensity of a Workout

Intensity is how hard you are working on particular exercises. The intensity of any exercise is important, as you need to place the right amount of stress to make a change in your body. Our bodies were built to be challenged and need to be challenged. For kids ages nine to twelve, it is best to use a perceived exertion chart. Intensity of the exercise should range from 6 to 9 on the chart at the top of the next page.

Remember: To improve flexibility, stretch before and after your workout.

Rate of Perceived Exertion

Value	Description
0	none at all
1	very light
2	light
3	moderate; starting to feel challenged
4	somewhat hard
5	hard
6	harder; body feels a difference
7	very hard; feel sweaty
8	breathing is harder; body is feeling challenged
9	very challenged; can still talk
10	very, very hard; hard to carry on a conversation

What Happens During Exercise

It is important to understand what happens to your body as you exercise. As you begin to move your body, your body releases energy-producing chemicals that keep you moving. Your internal temperature begins to rise and slowly raises the heart rate, increasing it from a resting heart rate to an active heart rate. Your joints become lubricated with synovial fluid to prepare your body for movement.

Your blood starts to pump oxygen-rich blood to the working muscles to provide energy for the movement. Your body begins to burn calories for fuel. As your body requires more fuel, it begins to take this fuel from carbohydrates and fat stored within your body. The longer you exercise, the more calories your body will burn. By increasing the intensity of your workout, your body will begin to feel sweaty, and you may feel perspiration. After approximately 15 to 20 minutes of exercise, you may experience a sense of lightness—what some people call a "runner's high." This is due to the endorphins (the feel-good chemical your body produces) released in your brain.

Around the 50-minute mark, your body may begin to feel fatigue, and your muscles may become tired. Of course, the time this takes will vary, depending on the endurance levels of your muscle tissue and your cardiovascular system. As you end your exercise routine, you gradually slow down, allowing your heart rate and breathing pattern to slow down, too. Your body will continue to burn calories for approximately an hour after you stop exercising. Of course, this also varies, depending on the intensity of your workout, the muscles involved, and your current state of fitness.

Motivation Can Come from Inspiration

Having the motivation to exercise every day can be challenging, especially for the tweens age group. But it only takes the right motivation to get these kids moving. We all have those days when we don't feel like exercising, but before you totally give up on the idea, take a few minutes for meditation. Clear your mind of "I can't" or "I don't want to…" thoughts and search for inspiration. Inspiration is not hard to find; it can come from anywhere: art, books, quotes, movies, music, religion, an idea, an activity, or even from another person.

One of my students told me she runs a couple of miles each day. When thoughts of quitting start to creep into her mind, she thinks of one of her closest friends who was in a car accident and is now in a wheelchair. She says she runs because her friend can no longer run, and that inspires her to finish her run. Another client of mine says he is inspired to work harder in his workouts because his mother is going through chemotherapy. "When I have weak thoughts I think of the strength my mom has to have for her treatments and her will to live," he told me. "So I am inspired by her strength to finish my workout." Open your mind to inspiration every day and make it a habit. To allow inspiration to work for you:

- Keep an inspirational journal.
- Listen to words of inspiration on your iPod while you are exercising.
- Read inspirational stories.
- Think of someone who has been an inspiration in your life and can't be with you now. Ask yourself, "Wouldn't that person want me to take the best possible care of my body?"

Inspiration and Exercise: Putting It Together

Without a doubt, inspiration can get people moving. But sometimes, when exercise and inspiration—or even just the chance to contemplate—come together naturally, the fit is stronger. You and the kids might try the following:

- Dance because you are happy and grateful for all the good things in your life.
- Jump rope and count out loud all the good things that are in your life.
- Run for a cause. Run for Breast Cancer Awareness. I find the T-shirts very inspiring when I read, "I am running in memory of…" or "I am running for ____, a survivor of breast cancer!"

- You don't need to wait to run in a charity event; every time you run or exercise, think about others who are less fortunate or need support right now.
- Run and pray.
- Exercise out of appreciation. Think about a person, a place, or an event that you deeply appreciate.
- Exercise with a smile on your face.
- Take your dog for a walk. If you don't have a dog, go to an animal shelter and volunteer to walk the dogs there.
- Think of the calories you are burning; feel them burning in your body.
- Exercise with the same intensity as the love you feel for someone.
- Think of a quote that motivates you.
- If a negative thought creeps into your mind, visualize your muscular strength deflating the negative though and kick it out of your mind.
- Exercise and chant, repeating your favorite mantra (for example, "I can do this; I can do this…").
- Experience the joy in every step you take toward a healthy lifestyle.
- Be an inspiration to others your age.
- Write a blog as an exercise journal, "I completed a 30-minute circuit training today. Here is my routine.…"
- Take a "before" and an "after" picture.
- After your workout, feel good about yourself! You completed a workout, and your body will thank you.

About the 303 Exercises and Active Games

How did the exercises in this book become tween approved? First of all, the exercises in this book were chosen because they are safe for most kids within this age group. Second, the chosen exercises challenge both kids' minds and their bodies in fun and creative ways. Kids are the best teachers when it comes to having fun, and these "fun ways" were designed by kids. They will repeat an activity that is fun, creative, and makes them feel good.

The physical activities included in this book involve different levels of intensity. They challenge children's muscular and cardiovascular strength and endurance through the use of playful competitions, challenges, and games.

How to Use the Exercises

Choose exercises from each category: stretching, mind and body, strength, cardiovascular exercises, sport challenges and drills, and active games. Use them in one of the formats listed below.

Adding Physical Activity

Start slowly by incorporating exercises into your current routine.

- 45 minutes washing a car + 15 minutes yoga
- 30 minutes playing your favorite sport + 10 minutes stretching
- 30 minutes household chores + 10 minutes stretching + 15 minutes sport drills
- 30 minutes walking + 10 minutes outdoor meditation + 15 minutes stretching outdoors
- 30 minutes shooting baskets + 15 minutes stretching + 15 minutes strength training

- 30 minutes bicycling + 15 minutes Pilates + 15 minutes meditation
- 30 minutes dancing + 15 minutes stretching + 15 minutes strength training
- 30 minutes performing water aerobics + 30 minutes strength training
- 15 minutes jumping rope + 15 minutes upper-body exercises
- 60 minutes doing homework + 10 minutes stretching + 15 minutes sport drills
- 30 minutes watching television + 15 minutes sport drills + 15 minutes vertical power
- 30 minutes preparing dinner + 30 minute family walk + 10 minutes meditation

Circuit Training

This type of workout combines exercises for many different sports into one workout. Stations, also referred to as circuit training, are commonly used by fitness instructors and personal trainers. You can take a variety of exercises or stick with one common theme and make the circuit a longer, more challenging workout. For example, to create a balance station, take five or six exercises, write the names of the exercises on a card, and place it on the floor. That becomes station number one.

Arrange all of the stations in a circle large enough so the players can move from one station to another and have plenty of workout space. Designate either a number of repetitions or a time allowance for each station. On the word "Go," each participant selects one station. Typically only one person is at each station, but you may choose to allow pairs of kids at each station. The participants may go around the stations for one cycle, or, if you choose, you can have them do it all over again. Any of the categories in this book will do well in a station.

Interval Training

Add a cardiovascular activity in between each station. For example, choose from:

- hopping
- kicks
- jumping
- running

Have the kids perform the cardio exercise for a period of time (for example, 3 minutes) and then go right into the movements for the next station.

Partner Training

Partner training is a great way to spend quality time with kids and exercise at the same time. It's a win-win situation. Choose a group of exercises and enjoy some active play. Better yet, get a group of family members or friends to exercise along with you.

Personal Training

People hire personal trainers so they can get a program customized just for them. With over three hundred exercises in this book, customizing a program for you and your tweens is easy. All of these exercises have been taught to tweens for years. Just read through each exercise and put together 30 minutes worth of the right ones for you and your kids. The rule of thumb is that if you want to lose weight, add more cardiovascular exercise to your program. To strengthen muscle, select from the exercises for the torso, upper body, and lower body. To improve your speed, endurance, and coordination, try sport skills and drills.

Always warm-up before you exercise, add stretching, add strength training, include yoga or Pilates, and have fun customizing your program.

Setting Goals

The following is a sample daily exercise plan. It uses a combination of cardio and body-weight resistance training.

Daily Training Guide

Day 1: Upper-Body Training

- Side Stretch (#4)
- Forward-Bend Stretch (#5)
- Standing Twists (#36)
- Close the Door (#90)
- Push and Touch (#91)
- Bent-Over Circular Row (#92)

Day 2: Cardiovascular Workout

- Yoga: Half Locust Pose (#25), Legs on Wall Pose (#27), Triangle Pose (#33)
- Walking Lunges (#182)
- Double or Triple Knee Lifts (#186)
- Step/Kicks (#190)

Day 3: Lower-Body and Core/Torso Workout

- Pilates: The Hundreds (#37), Tilt and Lift (#38), Scissors (#39)
- Front Kicks (#120)
- Roundhouse Kicks (#121)
- Squats (#122)

Day 4: Cardiovascular Workout

- Stretching: Head Nods and Neck Rolls (#1), Chest Stretch (#3), Hamstring Stretch (#10)
- Straddle Steps (#187)
- Heel-to-Bottom Jumps (#193)
- Run in Place with High Knees (#196)

Day 5: Upper-Body Training

- Pilates: Plank Position (#41), Roll-backs (#42), Swimming (#45)
- Triceps Challenge (#95)
- Biceps Curls (#96)
- Pike Push-Ups (#103)

Day 6: Cardiovascular Workout

- Yoga: Child's Pose (#18), Warrior Pose (#31), Chair Pose (#35)
- Run in Place with High Knees (#196)
- V Steps (#197)
- Pony (#198)

Day 7: Game Day

- Capture the Flag (#289)
- Dodgeball (#293)
- The Blob (#298)

Sample Weekly Circuit Training Plan

Here is an exercise plan I have used several times with tweens. Use this guideline to design your program, and modify it as needed based on your individual goals. For example, if you want to tone your legs and bottom, then do two of the lower-body training sessions each week. If you're looking to tone your upper body and build more muscle, do the upper-body routine twice and lower-body routine once each week.

Monday

Perform three complete circuits of the following upper-body routine with no rest in between the exercises:

- 10 Bent-Over Circular Rows (#92)
- 10 Biceps Curls (#96)
- 15 Incline Push-Ups (#101)
- 15 Triceps Kickbacks (#111)
- 10 Shoulder Presses (#113)
- 15 Forward Jabs (#117)

Once you have completed the weight-training circuit, do 30 to 45 minutes of intense cardio (i.e., treadmill, exercise bike, elliptical, etc.).

Tuesday

- Go on a 5- to 10-mile bike ride.

Wednesday

Perform three complete circuits of the following lower-body weight-lifting routine with no rest in between each exercise:

- 15 Squats (#122)
- 20 Side Leg Lifts (#126)
- 15 Standing Lunges (#127)
- 15 Mountain Climbers (#138)

Once you have completed the weight-training circuit, do 30 to 45 minutes of intense cardio (i.e., treadmill, exercise bike, elliptical, speed walking).

Thursday

- Game Day: Choose any game to play for 60 minutes.

Friday

Do 1 hour of Sport Skills and Drills:

- Mirror Image (#248)
- Shuttle Run (#255)
- Clock Pattern (#258)

Saturday

Perform three complete circuits of the following upper-body weight-lifting routine with no rest in between each exercise:

- 15 Biceps Curls (#96)
- 10 Pike Push-Ups (#103)
- 15 Lateral Raises (#108)
- 10 Triceps Kickbacks (#111)
- 10 Shoulder Presses (#113)

Once you have completed the weight-training circuit, do 30 to 45 minutes of intense cardio (i.e., treadmill, exercise bike, elliptical, etc.)

Sunday

- Go on a family fitness outing.

Keeping a Fitness Journal

Keeping a fitness journal is a good way of keeping kids committed to establishing an exercise routine. Fitness journals provide accountability, and to be accountable is an important step in creating a plan and sticking to it. Keeping track of an exercise program also increases an awareness of what exercises work to keep kids active. Kids can track their progress and identify areas in which they face obstacles, and together you can identify ways to overcome them.

Suggest that the kids can use a journal to:

- record the amount of time they exercise. Seeing the minutes of a weekly workout plan add up can help boost motivation. Set up a contract with tweens that offers rewards for racking up minutes.

- make and record challenges to friends and family. Challenge family members to see how many repetitions they can complete.

- track personal-best time or count their accomplishments in each fitness category. They can refer to the journal to try to beat an old record or track their progress to see and feel their achievements.

Varying the Exercises

Adding variety to an exercise program can improve adherence and can also help kids stay physically challenged and motivated to keep active.

Obstacle Courses

Create your own obstacle course by selecting some of the exercises from this book. Record the chosen exercises on index cards and then place them at stations either inside or outside your home. Transform the yard or living room into a free-for-all obstacle course. First, remove unsafe objects from the area. Collect any equipment you may need to complete the course, such as balls, a mini-trampoline, etc. Challenge the tweens to navigate their way through the series of exercises while being timed. Record all results and encourage participants to try to beat their own time.

Relay Races

Races are great exercise whatever your age. When engaged in a race, not only does a child get their heart pumping but the child also has to learn that even in the emotional excitement of an intense game or close race, she has to observe rules and regulations; to choose between fair or unfair, and to act on those choices appropriately.

When you have a larger group of kids (10 players or more), relay races keep the pace of the game moving. During a relay race, each team member participates in only a set part of the race, and he then tags another member of the team to continue the game until each player has had a turn.

Select any of the cardiovascular exercises in this book. Identify the starting line and the finishing line. On "Go," each player must perform the movement as fast as they can all the way to the finishing line.

Pyramid-Style Sequences

Select a series of approximately fifteen exercises. Have the children perform the first exercise. Then add on the next exercise and repeat from the beginning. Add on exercises until the full sequence includes all of the chosen exercises.

Choreographed Routines

Link chosen exercises together to create a choreographed routine. You can even add music to the workout to further inspire the participants.

Drills to Increase Sports Performance

Select a series of drills with which children can challenge a friend or family member.

Game Day

Kids don't realize that playing games is a form of exercise, too. Choose several of the games to play with friends and family members and let the sweat begin!

Key to the Icons Used in the Games

To help you find games suitable for a particular situation, the games are coded with symbols or icons. These icons tell you, at a glance, the following specifics about the game:

- the size of the group needed
- if a large space is needed
- if physical contact is or might be involved
- if participants will exercise on a mat
- if props are required

These icons are explained in more detail below.

The size of the group needed. Most of the activities may be performed with groups of any size. A few are designed for pairs, small groups, or the whole group. These exceptions are individually marked with one of the following group-size icons:

 = The whole group plays together.

 = Participants play individually, so any size group can play.

 = Participants play in small groups of three or more.

= Participants play in pairs.

If a large space is needed. A large space is required for some of the games, such as when the whole group is required to form a circle or to walk around the room. These are marked with the following icon:

 = The exercise may require a larger space.

If physical contact is or might be involved. Although a certain amount of body contact might be acceptable in certain environments, the following icon has been inserted at the top of any games that definitely involves contact or might involve anything from a small amount of contact to minor collisions. You can figure out in advance if the game is suitable for your participants and/ or environment.

 = Physical contact is involved or likely.

If an exercise mat is required. Many of the exercises in this book should be done on an exercise mat.

 = Players will exercise on mats.

If props are required. Many of the games require no special props. In some cases, though, items such as balls, jump ropes, chairs, or other materials are integral to running and playing a game. Games requiring props are flagged with the icon below, and the necessary materials are listed under the Props heading. Note that optional props will also be flagged.

 = Props are needed.

The Exercises and Games

Warm-Up and Stretching Exercises

All exercises are **any size** except as noted

Warm-up and stretching exercises are an essential part of any exercise routine and should never be forgotten. A warm-up exercise increases blood flow to the working muscles and prepares the body for the movements ahead. Stretching can take as little as 10 minutes and provides multiple benefits to the body. It:

- decreases pain and soreness after exercise
- improves circulation
- improves range of motion
- improves posture

- decreases muscle tension
- reduces muscle soreness
- improves your ability to relax
- allows time for mental training, such as visualization.

Warm-Up Activities

To get started, have participants spend 5 minutes on the warm-up activities listed below and then move onto stretching exercises.

Breathing

Teach the kids to always begin an exercise routine by increasing their breath. Have them follow your lead. Inhale deeply through your nose and exhale all the air in your lungs out of your mouth. Do this at least 5 times. If anyone starts to feel light-headed, tell them to stop and resume regular breathing. To increase energy in the body, have the kids try this deep breathing several times throughout the day. If they feel stress or want to relax at the end of the day, have them focus on the exhalation part of this breath work.

Slow Dancing

The first part of the warm-up should be moving each part of the body very slowly. Have the children follow your lead as you start with your head and move down to your toes, working every part of your body. Roll your head from side to side. Roll your shoulders up, down, and in circles frontward and backward. Swing your arms in a circle and then reverse the direction. Be sure to include bending your elbows and moving your fingers. Slowly twist your torso from one side to the other side. Swing your arms gently overhead and then down toward the floor, bending your knees and slightly leaning forward. Keep taking deep breaths throughout your slow dance. Step forward, backward, and side to side. Rotate your ankles and wiggle your toes.

Arm Circles

Have the children stretch their arms out at their sides, shoulder height. Lead them in circling your arms in one direction and then reversing and circling in the opposite direction. Create big arm circles and little arm circles.

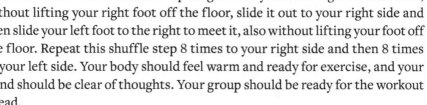

Marching in Place

With the children following your lead, begin by taking a deep breath in through your nose. Exhale through your mouth. Begin to march lightly in place. Gradually lift your knees higher. Keep your head lifted and your shoulders pulled back.

Tween Walking

Lead the children in walking to warm up. You can walk inside, outside, or even in place.

Light Jogging

As a warm-up exercise, a light jog will help increase the blood flow to the working muscles. Lead the children as you increase your speed slightly toward the end of your 7-minute warm-up.

Shuffling

Lead the children in a shuffle step. Begin with your feet together and then, without lifting your right foot off the floor, slide it out to your right side and then slide your left foot to the right to meet it, also without lifting your foot off the floor. Repeat this shuffle step 8 times to your right side and then 8 times to your left side. Your body should feel warm and ready for exercise, and your mind should be clear of thoughts. Your group should be ready for the workout ahead.

Stretching Exercises

Flexibility is the ability to move a joint through the normal full range of motion. Choosing a variety of stretching exercises from this chapter will help ensure that you and the kids are stretching all joints within your bodies. The following stretches can be used in the beginning of the workout as warm-up exercises and at the end of the workout as cool-down stretches.

Proper Alignment

Tell the children: Proper alignment for each stretching exercise includes maintaining a neutral alignment with the spine, keeping your belly button pulled back toward your spine and keeping your head aligned with your spine. Be sure to breathe throughout the full course of each exercise.

Sitting and Standing Exercises

Unless an exercise says otherwise, have children keep their feet hip-distance apart. If the exercises call for a sitting on a chair, be sure that their feet can touch the ground; if they don't, add a stack of books beneath their feet. Once they are seated, you can lead the children through the following advice about good posture. *Tell the children:*

- Your hands should rest on your thighs or at the side of your body.

- Round your back slightly, tilting your pelvis forward and flattening the small curve in your back, and then tilt your pelvis backward, creating an exaggerated curve in your back.

- Now find your neutral position somewhere between these two positions.

- Be sure to pull your belly button back toward your spine in each exercise to engage abdominal or stomach muscles. This also helps to protect your back muscles.

Warm-up stretches are important because they help to lengthen muscle tissue. This reduces your chance of injury because tight muscles tear more easily than warm ones. Warm-ups and stretches also increase your heart rate, which in turn increases blood flow; prepare the lungs to breathe deeper; and send signals to the working muscle groups that they are about to be challenged.

1　Head Nods and Neck Rolls

Tell the children: Gently roll your head forward to touch your chin to your chest; then roll it back, chin to ceiling. Repeat 5 times. Bend your head slowly to the right, bringing your ear to your shoulder. Pause and then bring your left ear to your left shoulder. Repeat 5 times and breathe throughout. Breathe deeply as you raise your shoulders as high as they will go and then drop them as low as possible. Repeat 5 times.

2　Triceps Reaches and Triceps Stretch

Tell the children: Reach your right arm overhead. Keeping you upper arm in place but dropping your hand behind your head, grasp your right elbow with your left hand and pull it slightly to the back and left. Hold for 15 seconds, making sure to continue breathing, and then switch arms. Raise your left arm and bend it at the elbow so your hand drops behind your head. Place your right hand on your left elbow and gently pull your elbow slightly to the back and right. Hold the stretch for 15 seconds and be sure to breathe throughout the entire stretch.

3　Chest Stretch

Tell the children: Stand nearly in a doorway, facing the frame. Place your left arm, elbow bent at 90 degrees, on one side of the door frame. Keeping your elbow on the door frame, turn your body to the right as if you were going to walk through the doorway. Doing this opens your chest and shoulder. Lean forward slightly until you feel a stretch on the left side of your chest and upper shoulder. Hold the stretch for 15 seconds. Switch sides and repeat the stretch.

4 Side Stretch

Tell the children: Standing on level ground, cross your left leg in front of your right leg, with both feet flat and your hands on your hips. Reach your right arm overhead. Bend your body to the left, pushing your hips slightly to the right, to feel a stretch along the right side of your body. Hold this stretch for 15 seconds and then repeat it on the other side.

5 Forward-Bend Stretch

Props A chair for each participant

Tell the children: Place your hands on the back of a chair. Slowly walk your legs back until your body forms a right angle. In this position, your back is nearly straight, as are your outstretched arms, and your body is bent at your hips. Press your heels into the ground, lift your buttocks toward the ceiling, and hold the stretch for 15 seconds.

6 Abdominal Stretch

Tell the children: Lie on your stomach with your elbows tucked to your sides and your hands near your head. Keeping your legs and hip bones firmly on the floor, press your hands into the floor and straighten your arms, lifting your upper body until you feel a slight stretch though your midsection. Hold the stretch for 15 seconds.

7 Wall Crawl

Prop A wall

Tell the children: Stand with your right side next to a wall. Slide your right arm up the wall in front of you as high as you can reach or until you feel a good stretch in your arm. Hold this stretch for 15 seconds and then repeat it with your other arm.

8 Cross-Body Stretch

Tell the children: Lift your right arm out in front of you at shoulder height with your palm down. Bend your elbow across your body at a 90-degree angle. Grab your right elbow with your left hand and gently pull your right elbow across your body and as close to your chest as possible. Hold this stretch for 15 seconds and then repeat it with your other arm.

9 Lower-Back Stretch

Tell the children: Stand, and with your right leg bent slightly, pull your left knee to your chest by holding the back of your thigh with both of your hands. Arch your back as much as possible. Hold this stretch for 15 seconds and then repeat it, pulling your right knee toward your chest.

10 Hamstring Stretch

Tell the children: Plant your left heel on the ground in front of you with your leg straight and your toes up. Putting your weight on your right leg, bend your torso forward from your hips and then sit back to stretch the back of your left leg. Hold this stretch for 15 to 30 seconds and then repeat it with the other leg.

11 Calf Stretch

Prop A wall

Tell the children: Stand about 1 to 2 feet from a wall, facing it. Touch the wall with the palms of your hands, which are extended in front of you at about shoulder height. Bend your right leg at the knee and take a big step back with your left leg until it is straight. Be sure to press your left heel down to the ground. Press your hips forward until you feel a stretch in back of your lower left leg. Hold this stretch for 15 seconds and then repeat it with the other leg.

12 Thigh Stretch

Tell the children: Lying on your right side with your legs stacked on top of one another, bend your left leg at the knee and grasp your shin or the front of your foot with your left hand. Keeping your left knee over your right knee, gently pull your foot toward your buttocks until you feel a stretch in the front of your thigh. Hold this stretch for 15 seconds and then repeat it with the other leg.

13 Bottom Stretch

Tell the children: Sit on the floor, curl your left leg behind you, and bend your right knee in front at a 45-degree angle, with the bottom of your foot facing your left thigh. Lean forward from the hips over your front leg and rest on your elbows until you feel a good stretch on the right side of your buttocks. Hold this stretch for 15 seconds and then switch legs.

14 Quadriceps Stretch

Prop A wall or something else to hold on to

Tell the children: Stand close to a wall and use it for support or hold on to a fixture. In a standing position, bend your left leg backward at the knee and use your left hand to pull your left heel up toward your buttocks. Hold this stretch for 15 seconds and then switch legs.

15 Wings of a Butterfly

Tell the children: In a seated position with your legs spread and your knees pointing to each side, bring the bottoms of your feet together. Holding your feet with your hands, slowly raise your knees up toward the ceiling and then slowly push them down toward the ground until you feel a stretch. Hold this stretch for 15 seconds.

16 Hamstring and Groin Stretch

Tell the children: Begin in a kneeling position. Keeping your left knee resting on the floor, raise your bent right knee in front of you until it is directly over your right ankle. Lean forward through your hips without changing the position of your right knee. Hold this stretch for 15 seconds and then switch legs.

17 Thigh-Abductor Stretch

Tell the children: Begin in a seated position. Then, with your right leg straight, put your left foot flat on the ground on the other side of your right knee. Reach over your leg with your right arm so that your elbow is on the outside of your left leg and you are looking over your left shoulder. Resting your left hand on the ground behind you, slowly apply pressure to your bent left leg using your right elbow. Hold this stretch for 15 seconds and then repeat it with the other side of your body.

Mind and Body Exercises

All exercises are

any size
except as noted

Mind and body movements are exercises that can actually alter your thoughts and stretch and strengthen your body through fluid movements. Most tweens who practiced yoga three times per week showed less stress and a better mood.

Meditation and Visualization

Children in other parts of the world commonly practice meditation, but here in the United States it is a practice that only recently has been accepted into our lifestyles. Meditation can be a healthful way of learning to control thoughts, anger, stress, sadness, and any issues that may be troubling you, or it can be a chance just to sit back and absorb the world around us. Work your way through the following passage and then lead the children through it.

To practice meditation, it is important to create an environment that is free from distractions such as televisions, cell phones, and computers. You don't need a large space, so even a meditation spot in your bedroom can work.

To begin meditation, start in a relaxed posture. This can mean you are seated in a cross-legged position on the floor, sitting comfortably in a chair, or lying down on a mat on the floor. It is not recommended that you lie on your bed because you may fall asleep. You should meditate every day, starting with 5-minute sessions and working up to sessions 30 minutes long.

Relaxing Meditation

Tell the children: Close your eyes gently and take several deep breaths. As you inhale, feel the air coming in to your lungs. As you exhale, release any stress you may have in your body. Notice your thoughts: As thoughts enter your mind, acknowledge them and then visualize them leaving your body.

Squeeze and Release

Tell the children: Begin in your relaxed posture. Inhale and then, starting from your toes, visualize each part of your body. As you do, squeeze each corresponding muscle group. Squeeze the muscles hard and then completely relax them. Move on to the next part of your body, squeezing and releasing all the way up to your forehead.

Using a Mantra

Tell the children: A mantra is a word or phrase that has special meaning to you that you repeat over and over again in your mind as a way to meditate. The most common mantra is the word ohm. You may choose any word or phrase that suits you; it doesn't have to make sense to anyone but you. Reciting this word prevents thoughts from creeping into your mind and can bring harmony to the rest of your body.

Attitude

Trying to maintain awareness with a passive attitude during meditation is perhaps the most important element in the discipline of meditation.

Tell the children: It is important to realize that thoughts will float in and out of your head while you are meditating. That is perfectly normal. Accept them and set them free and do not judge yourself. Most of all, keep a passive attitude about your meditation. With regular practice, your thoughts will shift and change, and eventually you will feel at ease with meditation. It is an exercise just like learning to skateboard. It may not be easy at first, but with practice, you will succeed at any skill you choose.

Prayer

Prayer is also a form of meditation.

Breathe Color

This form of meditation involves your creative imagination as well.

Tell the children: Begin in a comfortable meditation posture. Begin to breathe normally and then imagine two different colors. Imagine the color yellow, see it in your mind's eye, and now breathe in the color yellow. Breathe it in through your nose and feel the color yellow flow throughout your body, from your toes to your nose. Now think of another color. For this example, let's imagine the color blue. As you exhale through your mouth, breathe out the color blue. Feel it and, in your mind's eye, see the color coming out of your mind. This form of meditation can be used when you are upset or sad. You can choose any color that will make you feel better.

Inner Awareness

Tell the children: Find your posture and center yourself. Take several breaths, and then pick a part of your body on which you would like to focus attention. It may be a part of your body that hurts you like a toothache or a sore muscle, an area of the body where you carry stress and tension, or a part of the body that you never give thought to like your middle toe. Think about that body part, visualize what it looks like from the inside of the body, and visualize how this body part is connected to other parts of the body. How does it feel from the inside when you move this part of the body?

Outer Awareness

Tell the children: Meditation can also be practiced with your eyes open and your body moving. For example, take a meditation walk through the park. Breathe all of the smells into your body, empty your mind of all thoughts, and focus on nature. If you see a bird, become aware of that bird, imagine how it would feel if you were that bird, allow your body to feel yourself flying. Become aware of rocks. How would it feel if you were a rock? How does the grass feel below your feet? What would it feel like to be the sun, air, clouds, or a leaf falling from a tree? Allow your creative side to entertain your thoughts. Keep a journal of your descriptions.

Eating Meditation

Tell the children: Food is fuel for our bodies. And this form of meditation will give you awareness of the fuel you give your body. This exercise works best when you are alone or in a quiet environment in which you will not be disturbed. Sit in a meditative posture. Take full, deep breaths and bring your awareness to your food. Think about where the food came from. Think about the farmers and the work they provided to put this food on your plate. Become aware of every movement your body makes as you take the food from your plate and put it into your mouth. How do your taste buds react to this food? How does it feel in your mouth and how are your internal organs reacting to this food? Close your eyes and enjoy every bite of your healthy food. Your body will thank you.

The word *yoga* is derived from the Sanskrit word *you*, which means "to unify" or "to yoke." The practice of yoga involves seeking to "unite" and provide harmony to body, mind, and spirit. The practice of yoga can benefit you in many ways: It teaches you how to focus and concentrate; it also helps with breathing, meditation, strength, flexibility, and circulation. Breathing exercises can teach you how to breathe more efficiently. Meditation can help you focus and calm your mind. The physical aspects of yoga can increase your flexibility, increase body strength, and improve your circulation. Read through each description and choose 5 to 10 postures to practice 3 times per week. Change your postures every week.

18 Child's Pose

Tell the children: Kneel with your toes together and your heels slightly apart. Sit back on your heels. Keeping your neck in a neutral position, fold over at the waist and put your hands on the floor until your forehead rests on the ground between them. Be sure to let your weight rest on your heels and to relax and breathe. Use this posture whenever you feel you need a rest from other yoga postures. Remain in this posture until you feel ready to move on.

19 Cat Pose

Tell the children: Begin on your hands and knees. Make sure your hands are directly under your shoulders but do not lock your elbows. Spread out your fingers and then lengthen your spine by keeping your head and neck in a straight line with your back. As you exhale, tuck your tailbone under and round your upper back toward the sky. Visualize yourself as a cat stretching. Hold for 10 breaths. Repeat 5 times.

20 Cow Pose

Tell the children: Begin on your hands and knees, with your knees directly under your hips, your hands directly under your shoulders, and your back straight.

Spread out your fingers, and keep your head in line with your spine while looking at the floor. Inhale and look forward as you push your chest and bottom upward while letting your belly sink toward the floor. Hold for 10 breaths. Repeat 5 times.

21 Cobra

Tell the children: Lie on your stomach. With your elbows bent and your hands on the ground next to your shoulders, press the upper half of your body off the floor with your arms. Keep your legs and hips on the ground while your arms extend. Go as far as you can and hold the stretch for 10 breaths. Repeat 5 times.

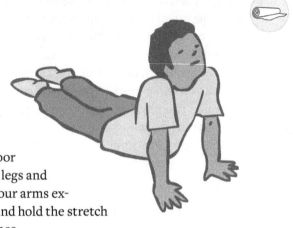

22 Incline Planks with Leg Lift

Tell the children: Sit on the floor with your legs extended in front of your body. Place your hands on the floor slightly behind your hips, with your fingers pointing forward. Press your feet and hands into the floor and lift your hips to form a straight line from your head to your toes. Keep your head held high and look straight ahead. Lift your left leg straight up as high as you can, flex your foot, and then lower it back toward the floor without letting it touch. Repeat 5 times. Do not let your hips sag. Switch legs and repeat the exercise 5 times.

23 Front-Lying Boat Pose

Tell the children: Lie face down with your legs extended. Stretch your arms straight out in front of you, palms down. Inhale and lift arms, chest, head, and legs off the ground. Imagine that your body is in a tug-of-war, with your arms being pulled in one direction and your legs being pulled the opposite way. Hold this pose and breathe for 5 breaths. Go back to the starting position and repeat the posture 5 times.

24   Tabletop

Tell the children: Begin on all fours. Slide your right leg behind you and lift it back and straighten it out at hip height. Do not sink into your left hip; keep your hips even with the floor. Slide your left arm out in front of you, keeping the palm facing the floor. Keep your head and neck in alignment with your spine as you lift your left arm to shoulder height. Hold the pose for 10 breaths and then slowly lower your arm and then your leg to the floor. Repeat 5 times and then repeat the posture with your other arm and leg.

25   Half Locust Pose

Tell the children: Lie face down with your legs extended. Place your arms alongside your body, palms facing down. Your chin is on the floor. Exhale and press your hips into the floor. Raise your right leg up, hold the pose for 3 breaths, and then lower this leg. Repeat this pose 5 times and then switch legs.

26   Single-Leg Bridge

Tell the children: Lie on your back with your knees bent, your feet flat, and your arms at your sides. Straighten out your right leg, keeping your knees aligned. Pull your belly button toward your spine, contract your left buttock, and lift your hips off the ground so that your body forms a straight line from knees to shoulders. Hold for 10 breaths and then slowly lower your hips without touching the ground. Repeat 5 times before lowering hips completely and switching legs.

27   Legs on Wall Pose

Tell the children: Sit on the floor facing a wall with your knees bent and tucked into your chest. Lower your upper body to the floor as you swing your legs up onto the wall. Your hips should be resting on the floor, not the wall. Straighten your legs but don't lock your knees; keep your feet hip-distance apart. Place your arms on the floor, palms facing up. Hold this pose for 10 breaths. Exhale and return your legs to the floor. Repeat this pose 5 times.

28 Mountain Pose

Tell the children: Begin by standing tall, with your feet hip-distance apart. Spread your toes. Tuck your tailbone under to lengthen your spine. Relax your upper body, allowing your arms to hang by your sides. Lift the top of your head toward the ceiling. Hold the position for 10 breaths. Repeat this pose 5 times.

29 Star Pose

Tell the children: Begin in a standing position with your feet farther than hip-distance apart and your toes pointed straight ahead. Extend your arms out to your sides at shoulder height, palms facing down. Relax your shoulders and tuck your tailbone under. Press your feet into floor and lift the top of your head toward the ceiling. Hold the position for 10 breaths. Repeat the pose 5 times.

30 Crescent Moon Pose

Tell the children: Begin in a standing position, with your feet hip-distance apart. Extend your arms out to your sides at shoulder height, palms facing up. Inhaling, bring your hands together over your head, keeping your arms straight. Interlace your fingers and point your pointer fingers toward the ceiling. Keep your upper arms next to your ears. Inhale and press your feet into the ground while extending your fingers toward the ceiling. Exhale and bend from the waist to one side, holding the position for 10 breaths. Repeat the pose 5 times to each side.

31   Warrior Pose

Tell the children: From a standing position, step your right foot forward, keeping your toes pointing forward. Bend your right knee, but keep your left leg straight behind your body. Inhale and raise your arms above your head, palms facing each other and fingers pointing toward the ceiling. Relax your shoulders. Lift your head toward the ceiling and hold the position for 10 breaths. Repeat with the other side.

32   Tree Pose

Tell the children: Begin in a standing position with your feet hip-distance apart. Shift your weight onto your left foot and bring the sole of your right foot to rest against the inside of your left leg. Be careful not to place the foot against your knee joint. Bring your palms together in a prayer pose at chest level. Inhale and raise your arms overhead, keeping your palms together and stretching through your fingertips. Hold the position for 10 breaths. Repeat with the other side.

33   Triangle Pose

Tell the children: Begin in a standing position with your feet farther than hip-distance apart and your toes pointed straight ahead. Turn your left foot inward 45 degrees and turn your right foot out 90 degrees. Inhale, and extend your arms to your sides at shoulder height, palms facing down. Shift your hips to the left and extend your upper body to the right. Exhale and, bending at your waist, lower your upper torso toward the ground and place the palm of your right hand on the floor outside of your right foot. If you cannot reach the floor, place your hand on your shin. Stretch your left arm up toward the ceiling, keeping your left shoulder back. Turn your head to look up at your left hand, keeping your spine straight and neck relaxed. Hold this pose for 30 seconds. Press your feet into the floor, inhale, and lift yourself back into the starting position. Repeat on the other side.

34   Downward-Facing Dog

Tell the children: Begin on your hands and knees. Tuck your toes under and exhale as you lift your hips toward the ceiling and straighten your legs. Exhale as you shift your weight back onto your legs and stretch your heels toward the earth. Relax your head and neck and breathe. Your body should be forming an upside-down letter V. Hold the pose for 10 breaths. Then exhale, bend your knees, and lower them back down to the floor.

35   Chair Pose

Tell the children: Stand with your hands at your sides, your palms facing in, and your feet slightly apart. Inhale and raise your arms overhead. Exhale, bend your knees, and press your hips back as if you were going to sit in a chair. Hold the position for 10 breaths. Repeat 5 times.

36   Standing Twists

Tell the children: Begin in a standing position with your feet farther than hip-distance apart and your arms at your sides. Inhale and raise your arms out to the sides at shoulder height, with your palms facing down. Exhale, bring your right hand down to your left shin, and place your left hand on your back. Hold this position for 10 breaths and then exhale. As you inhale again, come up out of the twist and return to the starting position. Repeat the pose 5 times and then repeat it, twisting to your other side.

Joseph Pilates, the originator of Pilates, was born in Germany in 1880. He designed a method of body control that called for conditioning, stretching, and strengthening the muscles within our "core" or torso area. Just like yoga postures, these exercises improve our flexibility and balance. Pilates helps you learn to strengthen your central core, using the abdominal muscles to control the movements. It then works to stretch and lengthen the muscles, allowing the body to become stronger and firmer without adding bulk. It teaches you to focus the mind as you exercise. The exercises gradually improve your coordination, body awareness, flexibility, and overall alignment. Pilates is said to improve posture as well because it challenges the muscles along the spinal column. The exercises developed by Joseph Pilates require concentration, so each exercise requires you to think about body positioning, movement, breath work, control, and resistance.

37 The Hundreds

Tell the children: Lie on floor, face up, with your knees bent and your arms by your sides, palms facing down. Flatten out your spine as much as possible so there is only a small amount of space between your back and the floor. Keeping your eyes focused upward, inhale. As you exhale, squeeze your stomach muscles and lift your right leg, bending at the knee until your shin is parallel to the floor with the right knee forming a right angle. Inhale, and as you exhale, raise the other leg too.

Holding your legs in this position, lift your arms off the floor, keeping them straight. Begin to move your arms in a small, controlled, up-and-down movement. Pulse your arms and count to 100. Then relax your arms and legs to the floor.

38 Tilt and Lift

Tell the children: Lie on your back with your knees bent, your feet flat on the floor, and your arms at your sides. Tilt your pelvis to bring your hips toward your ribs, keeping your back in contact with the floor. Hold this position for 15 seconds, release it, and then repeat it. Then lift your hips off the floor so that your body is one straight line from head to knees. Hold the position for 15 seconds and return to starting position. Repeat 5 times.

39 Scissors

Props A small-size ball for each participant

Tell the children: Lie on your back on the floor, with your arms extended above your head. Then place a ball between your knees, straighten your legs, elevate them slightly off the ground, and, while keeping your back touching the floor, rotate your legs so first the right foot is on top, pause, and then rotate your legs again so the left foot is on top. Repeat this set of rotations 10 times.

40 Rear-Leg Kickbacks

Tell the children: Kneel down on your hands and knees. Place your palms on the floor and tuck your toes under your feet so you can lift your right knee

off the floor. Tuck your head, slowly bring your right knee toward your chest, and then kick your leg straight out behind your body as you tighten your buttocks and raise your head to elongate your spine. Repeat this exercise 8 times per leg and then switch legs. Repeat the exercise for at least 1 minute.

41 Plank Position

Tell the children: Lie on your stomach with elbows bent and your palms placed on the ground next to your shoulders. Keeping your eyes focused on the floor, inhale and squeeze your stomach muscles, then exhale and gently lift yourself up onto your knees. Keeping your head and neck aligned with your spine, inhale again, tuck your toes under, and keeping your legs straight, push off the ground until your arms are straight. Keep your body in a line parallel to the floor. Inhale and exhale as you lower yourself to the floor and repeat 10 times.

42 Roll-Backs

Props A ball of any size for each participant

Tell the children: Sit on the floor with your back tall; extend your legs straight out in front of your body, hip-distance apart; and pull your belly button back toward your spine. Hold a ball (any size will do) in your hands and keep your arms extended in front of you at shoulder height. Exhale and curl your tailbone under as you roll backward toward the floor. Lower only as far as you can while keeping a curve in your spine. Hold this position for a second. Inhaling slowly, "row" the ball in toward your chest, exhale pushing the ball overhead, and inhale again, bringing the ball back to the starting position. Repeat the full sequence 10 times.

43   Reverse Plank

Tell the children: Sit on the floor with your back straight and your legs extended in front of your body. Place your hands by your sides, palms down, with your fingers pointing forward. Push down with your hands to lift your bottom an inch or so off the floor. Keeping your shoulders down and your elbows slightly bent, lift your hips until your body makes a straight line from your head to your toes. Hold this position for 5 breaths and then lower your hips. Repeat the exercise for at least one minute.

44   Rolling Like a Ball

Tell the children: Sit resting on your tailbone with your knees pulled in toward your buttocks. With your arms by your sides and your belly button pulled toward your spine, roll backward, stopping when your shoulders touch the floor. Then, using your stomach muscles, pull yourself back up to the starting position. Repeat 10 times.

Variation To make this exercise easier, hold onto your legs and pull up with your abs and legs.

45   Swimming

Tell the children: Lie on your stomach and extend your arms and legs so far in opposite directions that they naturally come up off the floor. Keep your spine lengthened so that your head moves up off the floor as you extend your spine. Keep your face pointed downward toward the floor.

Continue to reach your arms and legs out and away from your center as you alternate moving your right arm and left leg, then left arm and right leg, up and down in small movements. Count to 25 and relax, and then repeat the exercise 4 more times.

46   Reverse Roll-Downs

Tell the children: Sit on the floor with your back very straight, your knees bent, your feet flat on floor, and your hands grasping the backs of your thighs. Slowly begin lowering your back to the floor. Just when you reach the halfway point, cross your arms over your chest and hold the position for 10 seconds before slowly coming back up to the starting position. Repeat 25 times.

47 Breaststroke

Tell the children: Lie face down, with your arms extended over your head and your palms facing in. Lift your head and arms off the floor and hold for 2 counts. Then lower your head and arms. Next lift your head and arms off floor and swim your arms out to your sides and down toward your legs, thumbs facing toward the floor, in 2 counts. Repeat 10 times.

48 Full-Body Roll-Ups

Tell the children: Lie face up, with your legs extended, your arms over your head, and your palms facing each other. Move your straightened arms up and then down toward your feet, and pull your abs in. Roll your head, shoulders, and back off the floor and reach toward your toes in 4 counts. Roll back down to the floor one vertebrae at a time. Repeat this exercise 5 times.

49 Spine Stretch

Tell the children: Sit in an upright position with your spine lengthened and your legs extended in front of you and spread apart. Place your hands palm-down between your legs. Inhale and squeeze your stomach muscles, bend your head forward toward your chest, and curve your upper back. Exhale and stretch forward toward your feet, allowing your arms to travel forward. This movement should be done very slowly. Once you have reached as far forward as you can go, slowly roll back into the starting position. Repeat this exercise 5 times.

50 Knee Circles

Tell the children: Sit with your arms at your sides and your knees bent. Keeping your torso perfectly still and your knees together, lift your feet off the ground and slowly draw an imaginary circle in the air with your knees. Repeat this exercise 10 times in one direction and then do it 10 times in the reverse direction.

51 Backward Lean and Reach

Tell the children: Sit with your knees bent and your feet on the floor. Squeeze your stomach muscles and recline to a 45-degree angle while keeping your back straight. At the same time, rotate your torso slightly, moving your left arm behind you and your right arm in front. As you rotate, turn your head and look behind you. Repeat the exercise with your right arm behind you and your left arm in front of you.

52 Side-Front Kicks

Tell the children: Lie on your side and line up your ears, shoulders, hips, knees, and ankles. Reach your bottom arm straight out along the ground above your head and rest your head on it.

Rest your top hand, palms down, on the ground in front of your chest. Move your legs slightly forward of your hips. Lift your top leg a few inches. Flex your foot, swing your top leg to the front, and do a small pulse kick 5 times. Point this toe and bring your top leg to the back. Repeat this exercise 5 times and then switch to the other side.

Core-Stability and Strength Training

All exercises are **any size** except as noted

A person's strength usually refers to the amount of force that can be produced maximally by their muscles in a single effort. But for kids in this age group, we will be referring to strength as a combination of several muscles working together to perform a movement. Muscular endurance is the ability to work the muscles for a period of time without breaking form or experiencing fatigue.

Tweens love to challenge their own muscular endurance or to try to beat the number of repetitions someone else has done. Kids at this age can begin to use external resistance in addition to their own body weight. Light weights, bands, tubes, and lightweight medicine balls are all good choices. Make sure the children can successfully complete the exercises listed below without resistance first. Then teach safe and effective prop use before allowing the children to work with them.

In each set, the children should repeat the exercise as many times as they can until they feel muscle fatigue or they "break form." This means they have lost the proper form for the exercise.

As children become stronger, the number of repetitions (reps) they can do increases. After they can do 50 reps or hold a static movement for 2 minutes for most sets, try a more-challenging variation of that exercise, change the order of the exercise, or change to a different set of exercises for that muscle group. Do not rush through each exercise, and be sure to allow at least 20 minutes to do exercises from this section.

Core/Torso

The "core" refers to your abdominal and back muscles. Every movement your body makes starts with your core muscles, so it is important to work on strengthening your core every day. Choose five of these exercises and add them to your other workout program. Some exercises require a prop such as a mat, ball, chair, or broomstick.

53 Windmills

Tell the children: Lie face down with your legs and arms extended and off the floor. Tighten your buttocks and pull your belly button toward your spine. Exhale and pull your upper back up in order to lift your chest off the floor and then, balancing on the fingertips of your left hand, reach your right arm behind you to touch the back of your right thigh. Return your arm to the starting position and repeat with the other side.

54 Crossover Abs

Tell the children: Lie on the floor on your back with your knees bent. Place your left hand behind your head. Place your right hand on your left shoulder. Press your lower back into the floor and lift your left shoulder toward your right knee. Return to the starting position. Switch arm positions. Repeat this exercise 5 times.

55 Ball Twists

Props A ball for each participant

Tell the children: Lie face up on the floor with your knees bent and your feet flat on the floor. Place a ball between your knees. Put your right hand behind your head and your left hand on the floor. Lift your torso upward, keeping only your lower back and buttocks in contact with the floor. Rotate and press your right shoulder toward your left knee. Slowly lower your torso. Repeat this exercise 5 times and then switch sides and repeat.

56 Plank with Torso Rotation

Tell the children: Begin in the Plank Position (#41). Contract your abdominals and slowly lift your right arm up and behind you as far as you can while keeping your hips pointing toward the ground. Hold the position for 3 breaths and then return to the starting position. Repeat the exercise with the other side. Repeat the exercise 5 times on each side.

57 Ball Toss

Props A ball for each participant

Tell the children: Lying on the floor with your knees up and your stomach muscles held tight, hold a ball over your chest. Sit up and, as your rise, throw the ball toward the ceiling. Catch the ball and roll back down to the starting position. Repeat this exercise 5 times.

58 Crunches with Knee Rolls

Props A ball for each participant

Tell the children: Lie on your back with your arms by your sides, your feet off the floor, and your stomach muscles held tight. Place a ball between your knees. Bring your knees in toward your chest, tucking them close to your chin. Immediately roll your knees back to the starting position, hold, and then roll your knees to your right side, without letting them touch the floor. Hold. Bring your knees back up, roll to your left side, and hold again before lowering your feet to the floor. Repeat this exercise 5 times.

59 Long-Arm Crunches

Props A ball for each participant

Tell the children: Lying on the floor with your knees bent and your stomach muscles held tight, stretch your arms over your head while holding a ball between your palms. Lift your arms toward the ceiling and, as your arms come up, raise the rest of your body so that you are doing a sit-up. Arms should stop by your legs. Then start rolling back down, bringing your arms back over your head to the starting position. Repeat this exercise 5 times.

60 Arm-Assisted Crunches

Tell the children: Lie on floor with your knees bent and your feet flat on the ground. Place your elbows at your sides, point your fingertips to the ceiling, and press your lower back firmly to the floor. Crunch up slowly until your shoulder blades clear the floor and then press your elbows into the floor to lift higher. Lower your shoulders back to the ground. Repeat this exercise 5 times.

61   Back-Twist Extensions

Tell the children: Lie face down and place your hands on the back of your head, elbows pointing outward. Tighten your stomach muscles and slowly lift your right shoulder and your chest off the mat, keeping your left elbow on the floor. Twist up and back through the right side of your torso until your right elbow points up to the ceiling. Keep your head still and your chin down. Hold this position for 5 breaths and then repeat the exercise with the other side.

62   Leg-Up Crunches

Tell the children: Lie on your back with your legs raised up into the air directly over your hips. Place your hands behind your head and squeeze your abs to raise your head and your shoulders several inches off the floor. Hold this position for 5 breaths. Return your head and shoulders to the floor. Repeat the exercise 5 times.

63   Back Extensions

Tell the children: Lie facedown and place both hands as far down on your back as you can. Slowly lift your torso until your chest clears the ground. Hold the position for 5 breaths and then release it. Repeat the exercise 5 times.

64   Side-Kneeling Crunches

Tell the children: Lie on your left side with your knees bent and your left elbow bent in such a way that it is vertically in line with your left shoulder, allowing you to put your weight on your forearm on the floor while your fingers are pointing forward. Put your right hand behind your head. Contract your abs and lift your hips so only your left forearm and knee supports you. While your torso is lifted, extend your right leg and bend your right knee toward your right shoulder and your right elbow toward your right knee. Then straighten the leg and return to the starting position. Repeat the exercise 5 times, and then switch sides.

65 Can-Opener Crunches

Tell the children: Lie on your back and cross your left ankle over your right knee. Place hands behind your head and keep your abs tight. Slowly crunch your torso straight up and lift both shoulders blades off the ground. Bring your legs toward your chest. Repeat the exercise 5 times and then switch legs.

66 *V* Sit-Ups

Tell the children: Lie on your back with your arms overhead and your legs outstretched. Inhale and lift your arms up; exhale and, while lifting your legs up toward the ceiling, bring your arms up to meet your legs. You should be in a V-shaped position. Hold for a count of 5. Return to the starting position and repeat the exercise 5 times.

67 Rope Pull

Tell the children: Lie on your back. Straighten and raise your legs as high as possible, pointing your toes toward the ceiling. Imagine you are pulling yourself up a rope. Keeping your shoulder blades off the floor, reach your left arm up and across your body 5 times. Then repeat the exercise 5 times with your right hand.

68 Ball on a Swiss Roll

Props A large ball for each participant

Tell the children: Kneel with the ball in front of you. Place your hands, arms, and elbows on the ball. Slowly push the ball on the floor away from your body and into a full extension, hold the position for 5 seconds, and then pull the ball back in using your abs. Make sure when you push the ball away that you keep your back straight and your abs tight. Repeat this exercise 5 times.

69 Trunk Twists

Props A ball for each participant

Tell the children: Sit with your knees bent and together and your feet apart for balance. Lean back at a 45-degree angle. Hold the ball in front of you, keeping your arms extended. While looking at the ball, move it from side to side by twisting your upper body. Repeat this side-to-side movement 25 times.

70 Hip Swivels

Props A medium-size ball for each participant

Tell the children: Lie on your back with your legs up in the air, your knees bent at a 90-degree angle, and your arms out to your sides, palms up. Put the ball between your knees. Rotate your hips from side to side, allowing your knees to touch down lightly on each side. Repeat this exercise 5 times.

71 Bicycle

Tell the children: Lie face up on the floor, with your legs extended and your hands placed behind your head. Without twisting your neck, slowly bring your right elbow across your body while bending your left knee and bringing it as close to your chest as comfortably possible. Hold the position and then lower your elbow and knee back to the floor. Repeat, alternating sides. Repeat the sequence 5 times.

72 Forearm-Plank Knee Touches

Tell the children: Kneel with your knees hip-width apart and your forearms on the floor with your elbows in line with your shoulders, your hands clasped, and your head facing the ground. Extend your legs back, balancing on your forearms and the balls of your feet while keeping your back straight. Pull your belly button back toward your spine, keep your hips square, and lower one knee to the floor. Then straighten your leg. Drop the other knee to floor. Alternate knee drops. Repeat the sequence 5 times.

73 Lifted Reverse Crunches

Tell the children: Lie on your back with your knees slightly bent and your ankles crossed in the air above your hips. Place your fingertips behind your head, unclasped, and keep your elbows pointed out to the sides. Pull your belly button toward your spine, continue to contract abs to curl hips a few inches off floor in a reverse crunch, and hold this position for 5 breaths. Keep your upper body pressed against the floor, allowing only your hips to come up. Repeat the exercise 5 times.

74 Double-Leg Lifts

Props A medium-size ball for each participant

Tell the children: Lie down on your back with your legs extended. Place the ball between your ankles and squeeze it tight. Extend your arms out to your sides with your palms facing down to help stabilize your torso, and then lift your legs off the ground to a 45-degree angle. Holding the ball between your ankles, rotate your legs to the right as far as you can without letting your shoulders lift off the ground. Then return to the center and rotate your legs to the left. Repeat the sequence 5 times.

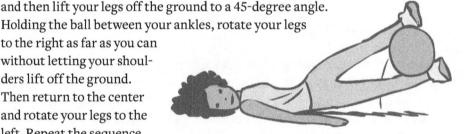

75 Abdominal Crunches

Tell the children: Lie on your back with your knees bent and your feet flat on the floor. Place your hands behind your head. Contract your abs to raise your shoulders and upper back 2 to 3 inches off the floor. Return to the starting position. Repeat the exercise 5 times.

76 Pointer Reaches

Tell the children: Start on your hands and knees with your knees under your hips and your palms under your shoulders. Keeping your abs tight, extend your left arm forward at shoulder height while lifting your right leg behind you. As you bend your right leg, reach your left arm behind you and touch the sole of your foot. Repeat the exercise with your right arm and your left leg. Repeat the sequence 5 times.

77 Side-to-Side Reaches

Tell the children: Stand with your arms extended to your sides at shoulder height and your palms down. Keeping your hips still, lift your rib cage and slide it side to side as if your body were in a tug-of-war game. Repeat the back-and-forth movement 5 times.

78 Seesaw

Tell the children: Lie on your stomach with your arms and legs stretched straight out. Reach around and have your left hand grab your left foot and your right hand grab your right foot. Lift up your upper and lower body and rock back and forth 10 times.

79 Half Camel

Tell the children: Kneel on the floor, knees are bent in a 90-degree angle, body in an upright position, (do not sit on your feet), toes flat against the floor. Raise your arms at your sides, shoulder height. Twist to the right and reach for the left heel with the right hand. Raise your left arm straight in front of you, just above eye level. Keep your hips and thighs perpendicular to the floor. Hold for 5 breaths. Return to the starting position and repeat the stretch to the other side.

80 Lower-Back Strengthener

Tell the children: Lie on your stomach, place your hands beneath your pelvis, and make a fist with each hand. Gently place your chin on the mat. Relax and take three breaths. On the third breath, contract your buttocks and raise both legs up, pressing your hamstrings, calves, and feet toward the ceiling. Try to hold this pose for 5 seconds. Repeat the exercise 5 times.

81   Side Plank

Tell the children: Lie on your side with your upper body propped up on your left elbow and forearm. Put your right hand on your hip. Pressing into your left forearm, raise your hips and thighs off the floor so your body forms a straight line. Hold this position for 15 seconds and then switch sides.

82   Add a Roll

This exercise is both fun and challenging.

    Tell the children: Lie on your stomach with your elbows bent and your palms placed on the ground next to your shoulders. Keeping your eyes focused on the floor, inhale and squeeze your stomach muscles; then exhale and lift yourself up gently onto your knees. Keeping your head and neck aligned with your spine, inhale again, tuck your toes under, and keeping your legs straight, push off the ground until your arms are straight. Keep your body in a line parallel to the floor. Inhale and exhale as you lower yourself to the floor and repeat 10 times. This is the Plank Position (#41). Now raise one arm out to the side and roll slightly backward into a Side Plank (#81). Return to the Plank Position and repeat the exercise on the opposite side. Repeat it 10 times.

83   Pelvic Lifts

Tell the children: Lie on your back with your arms by your sides, your knees bent, and your legs hip-width apart. Pull your belly button toward your spine and curve your tailbone under and up, tilting the pelvis. Slowly peel your spine off the floor, lifting the hips so they are in line with the shoulders and knees. Keep your ribs, shoulders, and neck relaxed, with the abs drawing in and up. Take 4 counts to roll up and 4 counts to roll down. Do this 8 times.

84   Pelvic Tilts with One Leg

Tell the children: Lie on your back with your arms at your sides, your knees bent, and your legs together. Contract your abs and curve your tailbone under and up, tilting the pelvis. Slowly peel your spine off the floor, lifting the hips so they are in line between the shoulders and knees. Hold this position and extend one leg, keeping the knees together and the hips even. Hold this position for 5 counts and then return your foot to the floor and extend your other leg for 5 counts, keeping your hips lifted. With both of your feet on the mat, slowly roll your spine back onto the mat. Repeat this exercise 3 times.

85 Side Leg Lifts with a Bent Knee

Tell the children: Lie on your side with your legs bent back at the knees at a right angle. Support your head with your hand. Keeping your knees bent, draw your abs toward your spine and slowly lift your top leg to hip height for 2 counts. Then lower the leg back to the starting position for 2 counts. Repeat 5 times.

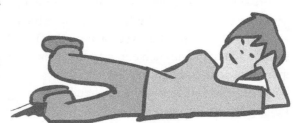

86 Supreme Fold

Tell the children: Sit on the floor with your legs extended in front of your body. Sit back on your tailbone, arms overhead, and bring your legs off the floor. Get your balance, raise your right leg up as high as you can, and then bring both of your arms down in between your legs. Lower your right leg and raise your arms back overhead. Then switch to your left leg. Repeat the exercise for at least 1 minute.

87 Prone Leg Lifts

Tell the children: Lie on your stomach with your hands stacked under your forehead, your shoulders relaxed, and your legs extended and pressed together. Draw your abs up off the mat to support your spine and protect your lower back. Bend your knees and, keeping your heels together, lift your thighs off the floor. Hold for 5 breaths before relaxing back into the starting position. Repeat this exercise 3 more times.

Variation Beats Lie on your stomach with your hands stacked under your forehead, shoulders relaxed, and your legs extended and pressed together.

Draw your abs up and off the mat to support your spine and protect your lower back. Keep your legs squeezed together as you lift them 2 to 6 inches off the floor. Without lowering your legs, quickly tap your heels together 20 times. Lower your legs and repeat this exercise 1 more time.

88 Broomstick Twists

Props A stool or mat and a broomstick for each participant

Before starting the game, make sure to move any objects that might get hit by broomsticks when children move them around.

Tell the children: Sit on a stool or on the floor. Find your neutral spinal alignment and then extend your arms in front of your body, palms down, and hold onto a broomstick with both hands. Pulling your belly button toward your spine, slowly rotate to one side. Rotate back to center and then rotate to the other side. As you warm up, you may gradually increase your speed. Repeat this sequence of movements 5 times.

Variation Place the broomstick behind your head and repeat the exercise.

89 Backward-Walking Crunches

Tell the children: Stand with your hands behind your head. Lift your right knee to your left elbow. As you lower your leg back toward the ground, step forward with your right foot and repeat the exercise to your other side. Repeat this sequence 5 times.

The following exercises will help to strengthen the upper body.

90 Close the Door

Props A pair of light hand weights for each participant

Tell the children: Stand with your feet shoulder-width apart and hold a weight in each hand. Extend your arms straight in front of your body at shoulder level, keeping your thumbs facing up toward the ceiling. Keeping your arms straight, bring them together in front of your chest with your palms together, still holding on to each weight. Then, with your palms still together, lift your arms straight up toward the ceiling. Return your arms to shoulder height and then to the starting position. Repeat this exercise 10 times.

91 Push and Touch

Props A pair of light hand weights for each participant

Tell the children: Stand with your feet shoulder-width apart and your arms extended down at your sides, and hold a weight in each hand. Keeping your arms straight, raise your arms out to the sides of your body and over your head, bringing the weights together so they touch, and then slowly return your arms to the starting position. Repeat this exercise 10 times.

92 Bent-Over Circular Rows

Props A pair of light hand weights for each participant

Tell the children: Stand with your feet shoulder-width apart. Holding a weight in each hand, extend your arms in front of your body. Then bend your knees and lean forward at your waist until your upper body is parallel to the floor. Let your arms hang straight down with your palms facing in. Keeping the weights parallel to one another, slowly circle them left and up toward your chest. Complete the rotation, returning arms to the starting position, and then circle right and up toward your chest. Repeat the exercise 10 times on each side.

93 Crisscross Reverse Flies

Props A pair of light hand weights for each participant

Tell the children: Stand with your feet shoulder-width apart, your arms at your sides, and a weight in each hand. Bend your knees slightly, lean your torso forward to about a 45-degree angle, and let your arms hang straight down with your palms facing in. Cross your arms at the wrists and raise your straightened arms out to your sides to shoulder level. Slowly lower your arms back to the front of your body, cross your wrists with the opposite hand on top, and lift again. Repeat the sequence 5 times.

94 Overhead Triceps Extensions

Props A light hand weight for each participant

Tell the children: With your arms extended over your head, hold one weight in both hands and keep your elbows pinned to your ears. Bend your elbows and lower the weight behind your head until your elbows form a 90-degree angle. Then press the weight back up to the starting position. Repeat this exercise 10 times.

95 Triceps Challenge

Divide the group into pairs or have the players choose partners.

Tell the children: Lie on your back with your knees bent and your arms straight above your shoulders, palms facing the ceiling. Your partner kneels just above your head and places his palms in the palms of your hands. Keeping your elbows pointed upward toward the ceiling, bend your arms at the elbows and lower your hands toward your ears. Then, while your partner pushes your hands toward the floor, try to extend your arms back up to the starting position, keeping your upper arms perpendicular to the floor and your elbows pointed toward the ceiling through the entire exercise. Repeat the exercise for at least 1 minute.

96   Biceps Curls

Props A light hand weight for each participant

Tell the children: Holding a weight in your left hand, rest your left elbow at your waistline. Bending your arm at the elbow, curl the weight toward your shoulder. Hold for 1 count and then lower. Complete 5 repetitions with your left hand and then switch hands.

97   Supine Triceps Press

Props A ball or light weight for each participant

Tell the children: Lie on the floor with your knees bent, and holding a light weight in each hand, bend your arms at your elbows so your hands and the weights are just above your shoulders. While holding on to the weights, extend your arms up. Then lower the weights toward your head, keeping your elbows pointed toward your knees. Hold the position for 2 seconds. Return to the starting position and repeat the exercise 10 times.

98   Shoulder/Back Squeeze

Props A pair of light hand weights for each participant

Tell the children: Stand with your feet together, your knees slightly bent, and your belly button pulled toward your spine. Hold a weight in each hand a few inches in front of your thighs, with your palms facing inward and your elbows slightly bent. Lean forward from the waist. Squeezing your shoulder blades and bending your elbows, lift the weights up until they are in line with your chest. Hold the position for 2 seconds and then return to the starting position. Repeat this exercise 5 times.

99   Wall Push-Ups

Prop A wall

Tell the children: Stand approximately 3 feet away from a wall. With your feet anchored to the floor, place your hands on the wall at shoulder height. Keep your body in a straight line from your head to your feet. Bend your elbows and lower your chest toward the wall. Then push away from the wall to straighten your arms. Repeat this exercise 5 times.

100   Bent-Knees Push-Ups

Tell the children: Begin on your hands and knees in a Plank Position (#41). Your body should form a straight line from your head to your knees and your arms should be straightened perpendicular to the floor, directly under your shoulders. Bend your elbows back, keeping your arms close to your body, and lower your chest toward the floor without touching it. Then push up to straighten your arms. Repeat this exercise 5 times.

101   Incline Push-Ups

Prop A set of stairs or a sofa

Tell the children: Begin with your hands on the stairs and your feet on the floor in a Plank Position (#41). Your body should be in a straight line from your head to your toes and your arms should be straightened perpendicular to the floor, directly under your shoulders. Bend your elbows back and lower your chest toward the floor. Then push up to straighten your arms. Repeat this exercise 5 times.

102   Push-Ups

Tell the children: Lie face down with your hands next to your shoulders, palms facing down, fingertips pointing forward, elbows bent, shoulder blades together, abs tight, legs straight, and feet flexed so your toes are on the floor. While keeping your body in one perfect line from the base of your butt to the top of your head and your abs tight, push your body up; don't sag in the middle and don't stick your butt up in the air. Use your chest muscles, not your arms, to lift your upper body, and use your core strength to lift your torso and legs. Look at the floor; your chin should be fist-distance from your chest. As you push, breathe out and lift your chest away from the floor. Once your arms are straight, don't lock them. Then slowly lower your body in a straight line. Keep your back relaxed and don't collapse into your shoulder blades. Lower until your chest is about 2 inches from the floor and then start the exercise over. Try to do one set of 10 full Push-Ups, but do only as many as you can with proper form.

103   Pike Push-Ups

Tell the children: Stand with your feet shoulder-width apart. Keeping your legs straight, bend at your waist until you are able to place your hands on the floor, and then walk your hands forward about 2 feet. Your bottom is pointing up toward the ceiling, and your body forms a V. Bend your elbows out to the sides and slowly lower your upper body toward the floor as if doing a Push-Up (#102). Keep your body in a V shape and move slowly to keep your balance. Then push back up to straighten your arms. Repeat this exercise 5 times, then walk your hands back toward your feet and stand up.

104   One-Sided Push-Ups   ..

Props   A small block for each participant

Tell the children: Get into a Push-Up (#102) position. Place your right hand on a small block. Lower your body toward the floor and then push back to the starting position. Repeat this exercise 5 times and then repeat the exercise with the block under your other hand.

105　The Pinch

Tell the children: In a standing position, extend both arms down by your sides with your thumbs turned outward. Try to pinch your shoulder blades together in back and hold for 15 seconds. Repeat this exercise 5 times.

106　The Lift

Props A pair of light hand weights (1 to 2 pounds) for each participant

Tell the children: In a standing position, hold a weight in each hand and extend both arms down by your sides. Keeping your arms straight, lift them up and to the sides until they are at shoulder level, hold the position for 15 seconds, and then slowly lower your arms back to the starting position. Repeat this exercise 5 times.

107　Crisscross Flies

Props A pair of hand weights for each participant

Tell the children: Lie on the floor with your knees bent. Hold a weight in each hand and extend your arms out to your sides with your palms facing toward your feet. Keeping your arms straight but not locked, raise the weights up over your chest, crossing your arms at your elbows. Hold the position and then lower your arms back to the starting position. Repeat this exercise 5 times.

108　Lateral Raises

Props A pair of hand weights for each participant

Tell the children: Stand with your feet hip-width apart. Hold a weight in each hand and start with your arms at your sides. Keeping your elbows slightly bent, raise the weights outward until your arms are parallel to the floor. Hold and then lower your arms back to the starting position. Repeat this exercise 5 times.

109   Prone Lateral Raises

Props A pair of hand weights for each participant

Tell the children: Lie facedown with your chin resting lightly on the floor. Holding a weight in each hand, extend your arms out to your sides, keeping your palms down and your elbows slightly bent. Squeezing your shoulder blades together, slowly raise your arms a few inches off the floor. Hold and then lower your arms back to the starting position. Repeat this exercise 5 times.

110   Rows

Props A hand weight for each participant

Tell the children: From a standing position and with a weight in your right hand, step forward with your left leg 3 feet and bend your left knee. Place your left hand on your left thigh and put your weight on that leg. Pull your belly button toward your spine, keep your back straight, and keep your head in line with your spine. Extend your right arm straight down, palm facing in. Keeping your right hand close to your side, pull the weight up to your lower torso. Repeat this exercise 5 times and then switch arms.

111   Triceps Kickbacks

Props A chair and a light hand weight (1 to 2 pounds) for each participant

Tell the children: Stand with a weight in your left hand. Hold onto the back of a chair with your right hand and bend over at the waist. Raise the upper part of your left arm until it is parallel to the floor. Straighten your left forearm, raising it until it is parallel to the floor. Repeat this movement 10 times on your left side and then switch arms.

112   Ball Pullover

Props An exercise ball and a smaller ball for each participant

Tell the children: Grasp a ball in both hands in front of your chest. Then sit on an exercise ball with your knees bent and your feet flat on the floor. Walk your feet forward until your torso, head, and neck are supported on the ball. At this point, your knees are still bent and your lower leg is perpendicular to the floor.

Contract your stomach muscles to stabilize your body; then lift the smaller ball up and back above your head. Hold it on either side with your palms facing in and elbows slightly bent. Squeeze your shoulders and then bring your arms forward and down until the smaller ball is back in the starting position. Repeat this exercise 5 times.

113 Shoulder Press

Props A chair and a pair of light hand weights (1 to 2 pounds) for each participant

Tell the children: Sit in a chair and hold a weight in each hand. Bend your elbows so you can hold the weights at shoulder height in front of your chest with your palms facing each other. Press your lower back against the chair. Slowly extend your arms forward and up. Return to the starting position and repeat the exercise 10 times.

Variation Chest Press. Lie on your back. Hold a weight in each hand near your shoulders, palms toward your feet. Contract your chest muscles as you slowly press up, bringing the weights together at the top.

114 External Rotations

Props A light hand weight (1 to 2 pounds) for each participant

Tell the children: Lie on your right side, with your right arm supporting your head and your left arm bent in front of your stomach. Grasp a hand weight with your left hand and position elbow against side and forearm across belly. Keeping your left elbow on your hip, lift the dumbbell toward the ceiling with your forearm only. Then slowly lower your arm back to the starting position. Repeat the exercise 10 times and then switch to the other side.

115 Reverse Flies

Props A pair of light hand weights (1 to 2 pounds) and a bench or exercise ball for each participant

Tell the children: Lie either facedown on a bench or with your chest over a ball, and allow your arms to hang down toward the ground. Grasp weights with both hands. Bend your arms slightly at the elbows and slowly raise them up and out to your sides until they are at the same height as your chest and you are contracting your shoulder blades as hard as you can. Hold this position and then lower your arms back to the starting position. Repeat the exercise 5 times.

116 Triceps Dips

Props A chair for each participant

Tell the children: Sit on a sturdy chair (or step) and grasp the seat's front edge with both hands. Maintaining a 90-degree angle with your hips, slide your buttocks off the chair seat while walking your feet forward slightly. Slowly bend your elbows, lowering your hips until your shoulders are in line with your elbows, and then push yourself back up to the starting position. Repeat the exercise 10 times.

117 Forward Jabs

Tell the children: In a standing position, balance your weight over your feet, keeping your elbows down at your sides and close to your body, and your hands, in fists, just a few inches in front of your shoulders. Extending your fists in a straight line out from your shoulders, punch your fists through an imaginary target. Alternate arms. Repeat the exercise 20 times.

118 Cross Jabs

Tell the children: This movement is the same as that used in Forward Jabs (#117) except that you will throw your punches across the center of your body. Keeping your knees soft and pushing off the ground with the heels of your feet, twist the hip on the same side as the arm you are using forward and rotate your torso. Alternate arms. Repeat this exercise 5 times.

119 Uppercuts

Tell the children: Begin with your arms at your sides and your elbows bent. Drop your right fist toward the ground so your arm is straight, and then quickly bend the elbow and bring your fist up and diagonally across the center of your body. As your fist comes up, rotate your torso into the punch and let your hip pivot slightly forward. Alternating arms, aim your fists toward your imaginary target. Repeat this exercise 5 times.

Lower Body

The following exercises will help to strengthen the buttocks, thighs, and calves.

120　Front Kicks

Tell the children: Keep your fists in a defensive position, protecting your face. Bring your right knee up and then extend the lower right leg into a kick toward your imaginary target. Do not overextend your knee. Return your leg to the starting position, maintaining balance throughout this exercise. Switch your lead leg. Repeat this exercise 5 times.

121　Roundhouse Kicks

Tell the children: Get into a side fighting stance by putting one foot forward and transferring your weight to that front foot. Come up on the ball of your front foot—a movement that will assist you in protecting your knee from torque—and, at the same time, rotate your torso toward your front foot and bring your back leg forward with your knee leading. Extend your back leg into a kick at your imaginary target. Return to the starting position, maintaining balance throughout. Repeat this exercise 10 times and then switch legs.

122　Squats

Tell the children: Stand with your feet hip-width apart and your toes pointing forward. Bend your knees as if you were going to sit back in a chair, slowly counting, "1, 2, 3, 4" until your thighs are as close to parallel to the floor as possible. Hold the position for 2 seconds and then straighten your legs to get back into the starting position. Repeat this exercise 5 times.

123 Starting Block

Tell the children: Stand with your right leg forward and your left leg behind your body about hip width apart. Bend your legs and place your left knee on the floor while keeping your right knee bent. Lean over from your waist and lift your hips into a "get set" position. Then straighten your left knee. Alternate sides and repeat the exercise for at least 1 minute.

124 Rear-Leg Lifts

Props A chair for each participant to lean on

Tell the children: Stand about a foot away from and hold on to the back of a chair. Keep your hips and shoulders square and pull your belly button toward your spine. With your right knee slightly bent and your left leg straight and slightly behind you with toes pointed, squeeze your buttocks and lift your left foot to hip height. Then lower your left leg to the starting position. Repeat this movement 10 times before switching legs.

125 Crossover Leg Lifts

Tell the children: Begin on your forearms and knees, with your elbows directly below your shoulders. Extend your left leg diagonally behind you, crossing over your right leg. Contract your buttocks and lift your left leg to hip height. Repeat this movement 10 times and then return to the starting position. Then switch legs and repeat the exercise.

126 Side Leg Lifts

Props A chair for each participant

Tell the children: Stand with your right side facing a chair. Keep your shoulders square, place your right forearm on the back of the chair for support, and lift your left leg sideways to hip height. Lower the leg to the starting position. Repeat this exercise 10 times before switching legs.

127　Standing Lunges

Tell the children: Starting standing with your feet together, take a giant step backward and slightly to the side with your left foot, keeping your heel up. Keep your right foot flat on the floor, your knee in line with your ankle, and your spine in the neutral position. Place your hands on your front thigh for support and keep your body weight balanced between both legs. Keeping your torso upright and your hips square, bend your front knee until your right thigh is almost parallel to the floor. Repeat this exercise 5 times, switch legs, and repeat 5 times.

128　Arabesque Reaches

Prop A ballet barre or tabletop with enough room for all participants

Tell the children: From a standing position, bend forward from the hips until your upper body is almost horizontal. Place your hands on a waist-high bar or tabletop. With your knees slightly bent, bring your right leg back until your toes are 12 to 18 inches behind your left foot. Keeping your knee bent, raise your right leg until your thigh is almost in line with your body, Straighten your right knee, lifting your heel upward 1 inch more. Rotate the knee outward and raise your leg another inch. Reach your left arm forward and upward, stretching from the fingertips on your left hand to the toes on your right foot. Return to the starting position. Repeat the movement 10 times before switching legs.

129　Open Bridge

Tell the children: Lie on your back with your knees bent. Extend your arms down along your sides, palms down, and raise your heels off the floor. Squeeze your bottom and lift your hips off the floor. Drop your legs to the sides so your

knees face out. Contract the muscles in your outer thighs and hips and hold the position for 3 breaths. Return your knees to the starting position and slowly release your hip and bottom contraction, bringing your hips and lower back to the floor. Repeat this movement 5 times.

130 Zipper

Tell the children: Lie on your back and extend your legs into the air, perpendicular to the floor. Extend your arms down along your sides with your palms down. Flex your feet, bring your heels together, turn your toes out, and rotate your knees out to the sides. Keeping your heels touching at all times, bend your knees to engage your buttocks and bring your thighs toward your chest for 3 counts. Then return to the starting position. Repeat this exercise 5 times.

131 Bottom Blaster

Prop A ballet barre or tabletop long enough for all participants to use

Tell the children: With your hands on a bar or tabletop for support and with your knees slightly bent, bring your right leg back until your toes are behind your left foot. Keeping your knees bent, raise your right leg straight back until your thigh is almost in line with your torso. Straighten your right knee, slowly squeeze your bottom, and then bend that knee, bringing the heel of your foot back toward your bottom. Lower your foot and then your leg until you are back in the starting position. Repeat the exercise 10 times and then switch legs.

132 Contract and Extend

Tell the children: Begin on your hands and knees with your hands under your shoulders, your back flat, and your head in line with your spine. Contract your abs and buttocks, round your back, and tuck your chin into your chest. Raise your right knee and curl your leg under your body while bringing your left hand under your body to meet your right knee. Then slowly uncurl your body, extending your left arm forward and your right leg back until they are parallel to the floor. Hold this position briefly before returning to the starting position. Repeat this exercise 5 times and then switch to the other side.

133　Single-Leg Side Squats

Tell the children: Stand with your feet a little wider than hip-width apart. Keeping your right foot flat on the floor, lift your left heel so that your body weight is over your right leg. Keep your arms relaxed by your sides, palms facing in. Bend your knees and lower your torso one quarter of the way down; your right leg should be doing the work, and your left leg should be aiding in balance only. Bend your arms and bring your hands together at chest height for balance. Straighten your legs and return to the starting position. Repeat this exercise 5 times and then switch sides.

134　Turned-Out Lunges

Tell the children: Stand tall with your bottom squeezed, your heels touching, your toes turned out, and your arms extended in front of you at chest height. Take one long step forward with your right leg, landing on your turned out right foot. Your right knee is bent slightly. Your left leg stays straight and turned out. Then, pushing off your left leg, sweep that leg through and step forward into a turned out left lunge. Keep moving forward until you complete 8 lunges per leg.

135　Swing Kicks

Props A knee-height stool or small chair for each participant

Tell the children: Stand behind a stool or a small chair that comes up to your knees. Put your hands on your hips and swing one leg up and over the object. As that foot touches the ground, swing this same leg back over your object to the starting position. Continue with the same leg 10 times. Then switch legs.

136　One-Legged Squats

Tell the children: Balance on your left leg. Lift your right foot a few inches off the ground in front of you and stretch your arms out in front of you. Keeping your back straight, slowly bend your left knee to sit and lean back 2 to 3 inches. Press into your left heel to return to the starting position. Repeat this exercise 5 times and then switch legs.

137　Split Squats

Props A low bench long enough for all participants

Tell the children: Stand 2 to 3 feet in front of a bench and put your left foot on top of the seat. Keeping your abs tight, bend your right leg and lower your body until your front thigh is parallel to the floor. Be sure to keep your left knee behind your toes and don't lean forward. Repeat this exercise 5 times and then switch legs.

138　Mountain Climber

Tell the children: Get into a Push-Up (#102) position with your back straight, your arms straight, and your hands directly under your shoulders. Walk your right foot forward, so that the knee is bent under your chest while your left foot is behind you with your knee slightly bent. Pushing your feet off the ground, switch foot positions, bringing the left knee in and extending the right leg. Repeat the exercise for at least 1 minute.

139　Figure-4 Squats

Tell the children: Stand up straight with your hands on your hips. Slightly bend your right knee and rest your left foot on it. Slowly lower your hips into a Squat (#122). Raise your body back into the starting position and repeat the exercise 10 times before switching legs.

140　Squat and Raise

Prop A sink or tabletop long enough for all participants

Tell the children: Hold on to a fixed object such as the edge of a sink. Keep your feet hip-width apart and your toes facing forward. Bend your knees and hips and lower your torso as if you are about to sit in a chair until you feel as if you would fall backward if you let go of the object you are holding on to. Keep your back straight, your weight on your heels, and your knees over your ankles. Hold. Press the ball of your left foot into the floor and lift the left heel as high as possible until you feel a contraction in the calf—about 5 seconds. Shift your weight to the right heel and hold the position for another 5 seconds. Push down into both heels to slowly return to a standing position. Repeat this exercise 5 times.

141 Inner-Thigh Lifts

Tell the children: Lie on your right side, with both legs straight and hips square. Support your head on your hand and elbow. Cross your left leg over your right leg and extend your right leg back at a 60-degree angle to your torso. Now lift your right leg as high as you can without rolling forward or backward, hold, and then lower. Return to the starting position. Repeat this exercise 10 times and then switch legs.

142 Single-Leg Calf Raises

Props A step for each participant

Tell the children: Stand on the toes of your left foot on the edge of a step, facing up the staircase. You may need to hold on to something for balance. Your right knee should be slightly bent, and your right foot is lifted close to your left ankle. Contract your abs, so that your pelvis is in neutral alignment, and keep your head and chest lifted. Then drop your left heel below the level of the step until you feel a stretch in your calf. Hold this position for 15 seconds and then rise up as high as you can onto the ball of your left foot. Repeat this exercise 5 times and then switch feet.

143 Step-Ups

Props A bench or step for participants

Tell the children: Face a bench or step. Put your left foot on top of it and keep that knee directly over the ankle with your foot flat. Press into your left foot and lift your body above your left foot until you can tap the edge of the bench or step with the toes of your right foot. Keep your abs tight and don't lean forward. Then slowly lower yourself back down to the starting position. Repeat this exercise 10 times and then switch legs.

144 Exercise-Ball Leg Curls

Props An exercise ball for each participant

Tell the children: Lie on your back with your heels on top of an exercise ball. Pull your belly button toward your spine, squeeze your buttocks, and lift your hips off the ground so that your body forms a straight line from your head to your feet. Bend your knees and roll the ball toward your hips. Pause. Then extend your legs, keeping your hips lifted the entire time. Repeat this exercise 5 times.

145 One-Legged Lifts

Props A ball for each participant; a wall, table, or chair for support

Tell the children: Holding onto a support with your left hand, stand on your left foot with your left knee slightly bent. Place a ball behind your right knee and squeeze your right heel toward your buttocks to hold the ball in place. Lean your torso forward so that your upper body is bent at a 45-degree angle from its original upright position. Keeping the ball in place and keeping your hips level with the floor, lift the back of your right thigh up and squeeze your buttocks at the top of the movement without changing your body position. Lower your thigh to the starting position. Repeat this exercise 10 times and then switch legs.

146 Kickbacks

Tell the children: Stand with your feet together. Swing your left leg behind your body into a kick. Keep your torso still and be careful not to use your back to help swing your leg. Repeat the exercise 10 times and then switch legs.

147　Bent-Knee Kickbacks

Tell the children: Start on your hands and knees with your head in line with your spine. Squeeze your bottom and lift your straightened left leg back until your thigh is parallel to the floor. Bend your left knee until your heel comes toward your buttocks, and then return your leg to the starting position. Repeat this movement 10 times and then switch legs.

148　Plank with Single-Knee Lift

Tell the children: Kneel on the floor with your knees hip-width apart. Lower your upper body until your forearms are on the floor, with your elbows below your shoulders and your palms clasped together. Balancing on your forearms and the balls of your feet, extend both legs back into Plank Position (#41). Keep your body in a straight line. Then, with your hips square and your abs pulled up and in, bend one knee to touch the floor. Finally, keeping your knee bent, raise that leg until your knee is hip height. Repeat this exercise 5 times. Release the position and switch legs.

149　Squat Pulses

Tell the children: Stand with your hands on your hips and your weight balanced on both feet. Contract your abs and drop your tailbone to achieve an upright, balanced position. Bend your knees at a 90-degree angle and hold this squat position while using your thighs to move you up and down only about 2 inches to make 8 little pulsing movements. To return to the starting position, contract your bottom muscles and push up. Repeat the exercise 10 more times.

150　Diagonal Leg Lifts

Props　A chair for each participant

Tell the children: Stand with your left side to a chair, your left hand on the chair back for support, and your right hand on your hip. Keeping both legs straight and your heels together, point the toes of your left foot forward and the toes of your right foot out at a 45-degree angle. Contract your abs so that your tailbone points down to the floor. Then squeeze your buttocks and lift your right leg back behind you, keeping it straight on a diagonal and lifting only as far as you can without changing the alignment of your torso. Lower your leg. Repeat the exercise 5 times before switching legs.

151 Seated Toe Lifts

Props A chair for each participant

Tell the children: Sit on a chair, lift the lower part of your right leg about 45 degrees, and rest your left heel on top of your right foot. Flex your right foot, contracting your shin muscle, and resist the weight of your left foot. Hold this position for 2 breaths and then relax. Repeat the exercise 5 times before switching legs.

152 Heel Lifts

Props A step for each participant

Tell the children: Stand with the balls of your feet on a step and your heels over the edge. Hold onto a railing with one hand. Lift your body up and down on your tiptoes. Repeat this exercise 5 times.

153 Wall Slides

Prop A medium-size ball or a pillow for each participant; a wall

Tell the children: Lean your back against a wall with a ball or pillow between your back and the wall. Your feet should be a comfortable distance from the wall, shoulder-width apart, and your knees should be slightly bent. Slide your upper body down the wall until your knees are bent at a 90-degree angle, directly over your ankles. Press your lower back against the wall and your heels down through the floor. Slide your body up and down the wall 10 times.

154 Wall Squats

Prop A wall

Tell the children: This exercise challenges the body without any movement. Stand with your back to a wall and your feet parallel to each other. Bend your knees to slide slowly down the wall until your thighs are parallel to the floor. Hold this position as long as you can. Repeat this exercise 5 times.

155 Wall Squats with Leg Extension

Prop A wall

Tell the children: Stand with your back to a wall and your feet parallel to each other. Bend your knees to slide slowly down the wall until your thighs are parallel to the floor. Extend your right leg forward and then put your right foot back down. Slide up the wall and then back down again, this time extending your left leg forward. Repeat this exercise 5 times.

156 Horse Stance

Tell the children: Bending at the waist, place the palms of your hands on the floor next to your feet. Pull in your belly button to stabilize your torso. Using one leg at a time and starting with your right leg, kick up. But don't kick up too high; you are not trying to go into a handstand. Your body will naturally come back into the starting position. Try to do 5 of these and then switch legs.

157 Ball Press

Props A ball for each participant

Tell the children: Lie on your back with your knees bent and your feet flat on the floor. Grasping a ball between your feet and placing your hands under your hips for support, bring your knees in toward your chest. Squeeze the ball with your feet and press your knees up and away from your chest. Then bring your knees back down toward your chest. Your movements should be small and controlled. Repeat this exercise 5 times.

158 Leg Circles

Tell the children: Lie on your back with your left foot flat on the floor and your right leg extended toward the ceiling with your toes pointed. Your arms should be at your sides. Keeping your right leg straight, rotate it from the hip in small circles. Repeat this exercise 5 times and then switch legs.

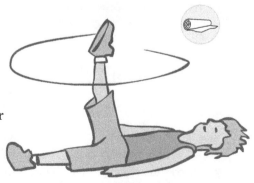

159 Leg Kicks

Tell the children: Lie on your right side, propped on your elbow and forearm. With your legs stacked and in line with your body and your left hand flat on the floor in front for balance, keep your torso lifted off the floor. Slowly swing your left leg forward as far as you can. Hold and pulse for two counts, moving your foot forward and back a few inches, and then swing your leg back past the right one. Repeat this exercise 5 times and then switch sides.

160 Bottom Strengthener

Tell the children: Start on your hands and knees. Squeeze your buttocks, bring your right knee toward your chest, and then, keeping your knee bent, push it straight back and up with your heel pointing toward the sky. Return to the starting position and repeat the exercise for at least 1 minute, and then switch legs.

161 Traveling Squats

Tell the children: Stand with your feet together. Step your left foot out to the side, sit back into a Squat (#122), but don't let your knees go past the front of your toes. Squeeze your bottom, stand back up, and take another side step into a Squat. Do 10 Squats in one direction and then reverse the direction. Repeat the exercise for at least 1 minute.

162 One-Legged Jump-Ups

Tell the children: In a One-Legged Squats (#136) position, extend your right leg straight out in front of your body. Squat up and down 3 times and then jump up into a balanced standing position. Repeat this exercise 5 times and then switch legs.

163 Jumping Jacks

Tell the children: Start with your feet together and your arms at your sides. Jump your feet wide apart, swinging your arms open, up, and above your head. Jump again, bringing your feet together and your arms back to your sides. Repeat this exercise 10 times.

164 Side Kicks

Tell the children: Stand with your feet wider than shoulder-width apart. Lift your right knee and kick your leg out to the side, concentrating on kicking through your heel. Bring your knee back in and return to the starting position. Do 10 repetitions and then switch legs. Repeat the exercise for at least 1 minute.

165 Lunges with Fly

Tell the children: Stand with your feet hip-width apart, your arms at your sides, and your palms facing in. Step your right foot into a lunge with your right knee positioned directly above your ankle. Raise your arms to the sides until they are at the same height as your shoulders. Lower your arms to your sides and return to an upright standing position. Repeat this movement 10 times and then switch sides.

166 Triceps Dips with Leg Extension

Props A step for each participant

Tell the children: Sit on a step or stair and place your palms on the edge of the step with your fingers pointing forward. Lift your hips by pushing down on your palms and pulling your core up, walk your slightly bent legs forward, and squeeze your shoulder blades together. Slowly bend your elbows and lower your hips back toward the step as you tighten your abs and lift your left leg to hip level, your hip will hover above the step. Hold this position for 3 seconds and then lower your leg back to the ground to the starting position. Repeat the exercise 5 times and then switch legs.

167 Hip-and-Buttocks Squeezes

Tell the children: Lie on your back with your knees bent. Extend your arms down at your sides, palms down, and raise your heels off the floor. Contract your buttocks and lift your pelvis off the floor while dropping your legs to the sides so your knees point outward. Press your outer thighs and hips open toward the floor and hold for 3 counts. Slowly return your knees to the starting position and bring your buttocks back to the floor. Repeat this exercise 10 times.

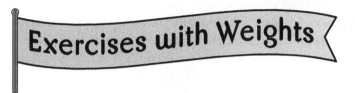

Exercises with Weights

The following exercises can be performed using light weights (1 to 2 pounds). Soup cans can be substituted for weights.

168 Scoops

Props A pair of hand weights for each participant

Tell the children: Stand with your feet together and your arms down at your sides. Holding a weight in each hand, bring your hands forward and upward to shoulder height while bending your elbows at the same time. End with the weights resting upon your shoulders. Now reverse this movement by extending arms straight out from shoulder height and returning your arms to your sides. Repeat the exercise 10 times.

169 Squats with Shoulder Lift

Props A pair of hand weights for each participant

Tell the children: Stand with your feet shoulder-width apart and your toes pointing forward. Holding a weight in each hand, and with your arms straight down in front of your thighs palms facing in, lift your arms in front of you to shoulder height. Keeping your heels on the floor and leading with your bottom, add a Squat (#122). Return to the standing position by straightening your legs and lowering your arms to your sides. Then squat again, raising your arms back to shoulder height. Repeat this exercise 5 times.

170   Lunges with Hammer Curl

Props A pair of hand weights for each participant

Tell the children: Stand with your feet together. Holding a weight in each hand, let your arms hang at your sides and keep your palms facing inward. Take a large step forward with your right leg. Keep your right foot planted firmly on the ground and balance your weight on both feet. Bend both of your knees, lowering your body about 5 inches, and hold. Then, keeping your palms facing inward, bend your elbows to curl the weights up toward your shoulders. Lower the weights and step back into the starting position. Repeat this exercise 5 times. Then switch leg positions and repeat it 5 more times.

171   Triceps Extensions with Calf Raise

Props A pair of hand weights for each participant

Tell the children: Stand with your feet hip-width apart. Holding a weight in each hand, let your arms hang at your sides and keep your palms facing inward. Bend your arms and raise them overhead so that your elbows are bent and pointing toward the ceiling and your forearms are pointing back behind you. Without moving your shoulders, straighten your arms to bring the weight over your head while at the same time rising onto the balls of your feet. Then, as you slowly lower your weight back onto your heels, bend your elbows and lower the weights behind your head. Repeat movement from this point 5 times.

172   Forward Lunges with Biceps Curl

Props A pair of hand weights for each participant

Tell the children: Stand with your feet hip-width apart. Holding a weight in each hand, let your arms hang at your sides and keep your palms facing forward. Step forward with your left foot, allowing your right heel to lift off the floor. Keep your abs tight, your chest lifted, your palms facing forward, and your elbows by your sides. Bend both knees until your left knee passes your front foot and your right knee points down. As you lower your body, contract your biceps, keeping your elbows at your sides while curling the weights up and in toward your shoulders. Use your buttocks and thighs to straighten your legs and push up out of the lunge while slowly lowering the weights to the starting position. Repeat this exercise 10 times and then switch legs.

173 Leg Lifts with Lateral Raise

Props A pair of hand weights for each participant

Tell the children: Stand with your feet hip-width apart. Hold a weight in each hand with your elbows slightly bent and close to your sides, palms facing in. Shift your body weight to your left leg and slowly lift your right leg to the side about 1 foot off the floor without rotating at the hip and while keeping your toes facing forward. As you lift your leg, raise your arms straight out to your sides, keeping your elbows and wrists at shoulder height. As you bring your leg back in, lower your arms and return your elbows to your sides. Repeat this exercise 10 times and then switch legs.

174 Squats with Arm Arc

Props A pair of hand weights for each participant

Tell the children: Stand with your feet shoulder-width apart. Holding a weight in each hand, let your arms hang at your sides, and keep your palms facing in. Lower yourself into a Squat position (#122), and at the same time curl your arms up to shoulder height and into a Biceps Curl (#96). As you return to a standing position, return your arms to your sides. Repeat the exercise 10 times.

Exercises Using a Towel

This is fast and fun. Just grab a towel and head to a wood, tile, or linoleum floor. These workouts use an ordinary towel.

175 Chest and Arm Stretch

Props A towel for each participant

Tell the children: Hold a towel in your left hand. Reach your left hand overhead and then bend your elbow so that your hand touches your upper back. Reach your right hand down and then behind your back to grab on to the other end of the towel. Gradually move your right hand up the towel and your left hand down the towel until you feel a stretch. Hold this position for 15 seconds. Repeat this exercise 5 times and then switch arms.

176 Side Slides

Props A towel for each participant

Tell the children: Stand with a towel under your left foot, hands on your hips. Sit back, bending your right knee as close to 90 degrees as possible while keeping the knee behind your toes. Simultaneously slide your left leg out to the side, keeping that leg straight. Finally, slide your left leg back to the center and straighten your right leg to return to a standing position. Repeat this exercise 5 times and then switch legs.

177 Backward Lunges

Props A towel for each participant

Tell the children: Stand with your right foot on the towel. Slide your right leg back behind your body, bending your knees to lower yourself. Be sure to keep your left knee over your left ankle and bend your right knee until it is almost touching the ground. Repeat this exercise 5 times. Then switch the towel to your left foot and repeat the exercise 5 times.

178 Front-to-Back Lunges

Props A towel for each participant

Tell the children: Stand with your right foot on the towel. Slide this leg back, bending your knees to lower into a Backward Lunge (#177), keeping your left knee over your left ankle and coming onto the ball of your right foot. While lifting your foot, slide your right leg back to the center and then forward, lowering into a front lunge, right knee bent over ankle. Slide your right leg back to center to complete one repetition. Repeat this exercise 5 times and then switch legs.

179 Hip Press

Tell the children: Lie on your left side, resting your weight on your left arm, with your right arm placed on the floor in front of you for balance. Extend your left (bottom) leg straight along the floor. Bend your right knee and place your right foot flat on floor in front of your left knee. Point your right toes toward your left foot and press your right hipbone forward. Press your right knee back 2 inches, rotating from your right hip and flexing your lower body. Hold this position for 3 counts. Release hip forward. Repeat this exercise 5 times and then switch sides.

180 Plank with Arm Circles

Props Two towels for each participant

Tell the children: Start in a Plank Position (#41). Your body should be in a straight line, supported on your hands and toes, with a towel under each palm. Hold your body still as you slowly slide your left hand in small clockwise circles against the floor. Repeat the movement with your right hand. Repeat this exercise for at least 1 minute.

Variation If a participant has difficulty making circles while balanced on her hands and feet, she can do a modified Plank Position (#41) with her knees on the floor and her body forming a straight line from knees to head.

181 Alternating Leg Extensions

Props Two towels for each participant

Tell the children: Lie on your back with your knees bent, your arms down at your sides, and a towel under each foot. Lift your hips 2 to 3 inches off the floor, press down into your left heel, and straighten your left leg. Then, while keeping your hips lifted, bend your left knee and slide your heel back up toward the starting position. Without stopping or dropping your hips, repeat the movement with your right leg. Repeat this entire sequence 5 times.

Variations

- For an easier exercise: Use just one towel. Slide your foot out about 12 inches, return it to the start position, and then repeat, keeping your hips lifted. Switch your feet halfway through the repetitions.

- For a harder exercise: Use just one towel. Simultaneously slide both legs out until they're almost straight and then bring them back in, keeping your hips lifted. Repeat the exercise for at least 1 minute.

Cardiovascular Activity

Cardiovascular endurance is the ability of the heart, lungs, and circulatory system to bring more oxygen to the working muscles and cells when challenged. This oxygen-rich blood produces energy for the support of exercise.

What is the best cardiovascular exercise for you? The one you enjoy the most. Most people think that cardio training is walking, running, swimming, and it is...but it is also any combination of upper- and lower-body continuous movements that elevate your heart rate and increase your breathing.

You can make your own "specialized cardiovascular activity" by combining 15 to 60 minutes of continuous movement. Listed below are some movements that will elevate your heart rate; link them together with other movements in this book and you have now created your own cardio workout. You can choose from several mini-combinations or combine some of your favorite movements with intervals of cardio such as running, walking, and Squat Jumping Jacks (#211). You can also do these movements while traveling in different directions to increase your heart rate. Here is an example of a simple aerobic dance class routine. Notice how it is only a series of exercises linked together.

Easy Aerobic Dance

- In a standing position roll shoulders, and do Biceps Curls (#96) forward and backward to prepare your body for a workout.
- Walk forward 8 steps.
- Travel backward 8 steps using various arm movements.
- Repeat each of the previous movements 2 more times.
- Travel forward 8 steps, leading with your right foot.
- Do 2 Straddle Steps (#187) in place.
- Do 4 Step-Kicks (#190).
- Do 2 Heel-to-Bottom Jumps (#193).

Repeat the entire sequence from the beginning. Add on:

- Walk backward 8 steps.
- Do an in-place Triple Knee Lift (#186) using your right knee.
- Do an in-place Triple Knee Lift (#186) using your left knee.
- Walk forward 8 steps.

Repeat the entire sequence. Add on:

- Do 8 Step/Kicks (#190), alternating legs.
- Do 8 Backward Lunges (#177), alternating legs.

Repeat the entire sequence 4 times.

Kickboxing Routine

- Jump rope in place without rope 32 times.
- Do 4 right Forward Jabs (#117).
- Do 4 left Forward Jabs (#117).
- Do 8 alternating punches.
- Do 4 alternating Front Kicks (#120).
- Do 4 Side Kicks (#164), right side.
- Do 4 alternating Front Kicks (#120).
- Do 4 Side Kicks (#164), left side.
- Jump rope in place without rope 32 times.

Repeat the previous sequence.

- Do 4 Uppercuts (#119).
- Do 4 One-Legged Squats (#136).
- Do 4 alternating Front Kicks (#120).
- Do 4 Squat Jumping Jacks (#211).
- Jump rope travel without rope 32 times.

Repeat the previous sequence.

- Do 4 Squat Jumping Jacks (#211) with alternating Forward Jabs (#117).
- Shuffle Step (#189) to the right 4 times, followed by 4 punches.
- Shuffle Step (#189) to the left 4 times, followed by 4 punches.
- Do 4 Single-Leg Rebounds (#209).
- Punch a speed bag 32 times.

Repeat the previous sequence 4 times.

It is very easy to pull together a cardiovascular routine. If you change the style to kickboxing, substitute some martial arts movements from the book for some of the movements listed above. You can make it any style you feel comfortable doing. Just pick out several movements and try to keep them in 8-count blocks of movement. If you keep each new add-on to 4 sections, you can add music to your routine.

Movements to Pump Up Your Heart Rate

The following exercises include the use of upper- and lower-body movements. If you have participants travel these movements, it will increase the intensity of their heart rates. All of the following movements can be traveled forward, backward, side to side, or on a diagonal. Be creative: combine some of the movements below with movements from elsewhere in this book. Design your own 15- or 30-minute workout.

182 Walking Lunges

Tell the children: Just as the name implies, you will be walking while performing this exercise. Take a big step forward and lower down into a Standing Lunge (#127). Rather than pushing off with your front foot to return to the upright position, push off with your rear foot, moving it up until both of your feet are side by side. Take the next step with the opposite foot and continue the movement 10 times.

183 Charleston

Tell the children: From a standing position, step forward with your right foot and then swing your left foot forward to a kick. Immediately bring your left foot behind your right foot and transfer your weight onto your left foot. Pick up your right foot, swing it behind your left foot, tapping your right toes behind your left foot, and then immediately step forward with your right foot. Repeat the entire sequence 10 times. To challenge your coordination, try leading off with the opposite foot and repeat the sequence 10 times.

184 Grapevine

Tell the children: From a standing position, step to the right side with your right foot. Bring your left foot slightly behind and past your right foot. Take another step to your right side with your right foot and bring your left foot alongside your right foot. Repeat this exercise 5 times and then reverse direction.

185 Figure 8s

Tell the children: In a standing position with your feet hip-distance apart, press your right hip forward and around, then press your left hip forward and around. Like the name implies, you should be creating a figure 8 with your hips. Repeat this exercise 5 times.

186 Double or Triple Knee Lifts

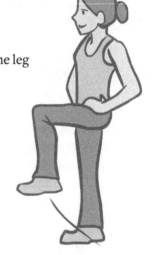

Tell the children: From a standing position, bend one leg and raise that knee until it is at hip height. Return your leg to the starting position and tap the floor lightly with your foot. Raise the same knee back to hip height. Return your leg to the starting position and tap the floor lightly with your foot. (This ends the double.) Raise the same knee back to hip height. Return your leg to the starting position. (This ends the triple.) Repeat this exercise 5 times and then switch legs.

187 Straddle Steps

Tell the children: Standing with your feet together, step wide with your right leg and then step wide with your left leg. Immediately bring your right leg back to the starting position and then bring your left leg back to the starting position. Repeat this sequence 10 times. This movement can be done slowly or quickly.

188 Step Touch

Tell the children: From a standing position, step your right foot out to your right side. Immediately bend your left leg and move your left foot so your toes touch lightly next to your right foot. Do not transfer your weight onto your left foot. Instead, immediately step your left foot out to your left side and move your right foot so your right toes touch lightly next to your left foot. Repeat this movement side to side 10 times. This movement can be traveled around the room.

189   Shuffle Steps

Tell the children: From a standing position, turn slightly to your left. Step your right foot out on a right diagonal and slide your left foot to meet it. Immediately turn your body to the right diagonal and step your left foot out on a left diagonal and slide your right foot to meet it. Repeat this exercise 5 times.

190   Step/Kicks

Tell the children: Stand with your feet hip-width apart and your hands on your hips. Step forward with your left foot and immediately kick your right leg straight in front of your body into a step forward. Then repeat the movement with your left leg. Repeat the exercise 10 times with each leg.

191   Side Lunges/Knee Lifts

Tell the children: Begin in a side-lunge position by stepping out with your right leg, bending your right knee to a 45-degree angle and making sure to keep your knee behind your toes, and stretching out your left leg while keeping your upper body still. Squeeze your buttocks and shift your weight to your right side and lift your left knee toward your right elbow. Return to the starting position and repeat this sequence 10 times before switching to the other leg.

192   Toe-Touch Kicks

Tell the children: Stand with your feet shoulder-width apart and your arms reaching overhead. Swing one leg forward into a kick and bring your hands down to meet your toes. Then, as you lower your leg into the starting position, raise your arms back overhead. Alternate the leg with which you kick. Repeat the whole movement 10 times.

193   Heel-to-Bottom Jumps

Tell the children: From a standing position, bend your knees slightly and jump up in such a way that you kick the back of your thighs or bottom with your heels. Repeat this movement 10 times without stopping.

194 Jogging

Tell the children: Your body moves in many different directions, not just forward and backward. Jog sideways to the left—leading with your left leg and without crossing your legs—as far as you can go without bumping into a wall or object for 1 minute, then repeat the exercise moving to the right and leading with your right leg for 1 minute.

195 Speed Walk

Tell the children: Walk as quickly as you can in place. If you have a lot of space or can go outside, travel forward and backward. Walk for 1 minute.

196 Run in Place with High Knees

Tell the children: Run in place. Slowly bring your knees up to waist height but don't bring them any higher than that. Run for 1 minute.

197 *V* Steps

Tell the children: Stand with your feet together. Step your right foot out to the right side and immediately step your left foot out to the left side. Your legs should be in a wide stance at this point. Next step your right foot back to the starting position and do the same with your left foot. This movement can be done quickly or slowly. Repeat this exercise 10 times, leading with your right foot, and then switch feet.

198 Pony

Tell the children: From a standing position, jump to the right side with your right foot and allow your left foot to follow your right foot, but instead of placing it down on the floor, simply tap the floor with your toe. Then immediately jump to the left side with your left foot and allow your right foot to follow the left and tap the floor next to it. Repeat this movement for 1 minute.

Variations

- Add a second jump to each side after the single jumps.
- Have the participants raise their arms in the air as they jump.

199 Squats and Side Lifts

Props A chair for each participant

Tell the children: Stand with your feet shoulder-width apart. With your hand on a chair for balance, point your toes outward slightly. Bending slowly at the knees and hips, do a Squat (#122) as though sitting in a chair. Keep your back straight and don't allow your knees to extend beyond your toes. Stop when your thighs are parallel to the floor. Hold this position for 3 seconds and then return to the starting position. Immediately swing your right leg up to your right side. Return to a squat position and now alternate by raising your left leg into a side leg lift. Repeat this entire movement 10 times.

200 Circle-Arm Squats

Tell the children: Stand with your feet wide and angled diagonally outward and your arms hanging down in front of you. Squat (#122), keeping your knees behind your toes. Circle both of your arms to the right, up overhead, and then toward the left. Then straighten your right knee and lift your bent left knee to meet your left elbow. Unwind your arms in the opposite direction as you return to a squat position. Repeat on the other side. Continue exercise for at least 1 minute.

201 Standing Knee Crossovers

Tell the children: Stand with your arms out front. Keep your upper arms level with your shoulders and bend your elbows to a 45-degree angle. Bring your right knee up toward your left elbow until they touch. Then return your arm and leg back to the starting position. Repeat the exercise with your left knee and right elbow. Repeat this exercise 10 times.

202 Skater Lunges

Tell the children: Stand with your feet shoulder-width apart and your arms up overhead. Step your right leg diagonally back behind your left and lower into a Backward Lunge (#177), bringing your arms down in front of your body. Return to the starting position and reach your arms back over your head. Repeat the exercise but step back with your other leg. Continue the exercise for at least 1 minute.

Vertical-Power Training

Vertical training is used by coaches and personal trainers around the world to improve sports performance in athletes. Vertical training is a series of fast and powerful movements that will help to increase your speed, jumps, coordination, hitting, throwing, and endurance.

The following movements do not need any special equipment. Body weight and muscle is enough to use with kids at this age. These exercises are also fun to do on a trampoline or in a swimming pool. Vertical power exercises develop power in any sport that involves strong, powerful movement of the legs. As you and your tweens are doing these exercises, you will feel your heart and lungs being challenged as well as your legs. Because these exercises require a great deal of strength, they are listed in order from the least challenging to the most challenging. Emphasize for the kids that they should stop doing each exercise when they can't do another repetition successfully and with control.

203   Overhead Throws

Props A medium-size ball for each participant; a wall

Tell the children: Stand facing a wall and holding the ball with both hands over your head. Throw it as hard as you can at the wall, let the ball bounce once on its way back to you, and then catch it with both hands. Repeat this exercise 5 times.

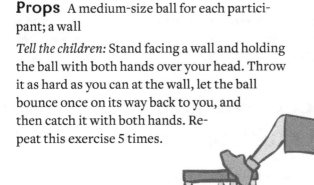

204 Side Throws

Props A medium-size ball for each participant; a wall

Tell the children: Standing sideways to a wall, hold the ball with both hands. Twist at your waist and throw the ball at the wall as hard as you can while still maintaining control. Try to catch the ball without letting it bounce. Repeat this exercise several times, alternating the side you twist and throw toward. Repeat this exercise 5 times.

205 Slams

Props A medium-size ball for each participant

Tell the children: Stand and hold a ball overhead in both of your hands. Then forcefully throw the ball down at the floor and catch it on the first bounce. Repeat this exercise 5 times.

206 Skipping

Tell the children: From a standing position, bend and lift your right knee toward your chest while hopping forward on your left leg and lowering the right knee back toward the starting position. Then, without stopping, alternate legs and complete the same movement. Repeat full movement for 3 minutes.

Variation If the participants are having a difficult time, have them use a 2-count jump to help them get the rhythm: Lift knee and hop, hop with feet together, and then switch legs.

207 Advanced Mountain Climber with Speed

Tell the children: Assume a Plank Position (#41). Keeping your abs tight and your hips level, pull your right knee toward your chest and then extend your right leg back to the starting position. Repeat the action with your left leg. Once you are comfortable with this motion, move your legs as quickly as you can 8 times, come up into a jump up position, and then drop back into a mountain-climber position for 8 more quick repetitions. Repeat this entire sequence 5 times.

208   Vertical Depth Jumps

Props A step or a sturdy box for each participant

Tell the children: Jump from the bottom step (or a sturdy box) to the ground, landing on both feet. Then immediately jump straight up while reaching up with both hands. Step back up on the box and start again. Repeat the exercise 10 times.

209   Single-Leg Rebounds

Tell the children: Begin by standing on one leg. Bend the other leg at the knee and pull your heel toward your bottom. Bend the leg you are standing on to lower your body and then jump up high—with control—landing back on the same leg. Repeat the exercise with this leg 5 times and then switch legs.

210   Leaping

Tell the children: Begin by pushing off with one leg and leaping forward. Repeat, leading with the same leg. When you feel fatigue in the first leg, switch and let the other leg lead.

Variation Alternate the lead leg each time while leaping. Try to get some height. Leap, alternating legs, for 1 minute.

211   Squat Jumping Jacks

Tell the children: Go into a very-low Squat (#122) position and then perform 3 Jumping Jacks (#163), keeping the Squat position. On the fourth count, come up for one more regular Jumping Jack. Repeat this exercise 5 times.

212   Rebound Running

Tell the children: Imagine running on the moon, where gravity doesn't pull you down. Now focus on pushing upward each time you run to try to mimic that effect. Try to get higher each time you take a step. Run for 1 minute.

213 Simulated Step Jump-Ups

Props A step for each participant

Tell the children: Stand facing a sturdy step with your feet hip-width apart and your arms at your sides. Keeping your right foot on the floor or lower step, bend and raise your left leg and place your left foot in the middle of the step. Keep your weight evenly distributed over the balls of your feet. Then, pushing off with your feet, jump straight up as high as you can and raise your arms over your head. As you push up with your left thigh, extend your right leg behind you, toes pointed, and squeeze your buttocks. Return to the starting position and lower your arms back to your sides. Repeat this exercise 10 times.

214 Side Skip-Ups

Props A step for each participant

Tell the children: Stand tall with your left foot firmly on a step and your right foot one step lower. Bend your knees, pull your belly button toward your spine, and shift your body weight to the ball of your left foot. Now skip, pushing off with your left foot, jumping straight up, and bending your right knee at the top of the jump. Swing your bent left arm forward with the right knee. Land with your left foot on one step and your right foot on the ground. Do as many of these as you can on one side then repeat the movement on the other side.

215 Power Jump-Ups

Tell the children: Stand with your feet hip-width apart, your elbows bent, and your hands at your sides. Bend your knees and sit down into a Squat (#122). Then jump as high as you can by quickly straightening your legs and swinging your arms forward and up to create momentum. Land with bent knees and lower your hips into a Squat to neutralize the impact. Repeat this exercise 5 times.

216 Squat-Thrust-Jump Rocket

Tell the children: Stand with your feet shoulder-width apart, your shoulders back, and your abs tight. Shift your body weight onto your heels and lower yourself into a deep Squat (#122) until your thighs are parallel to the floor. Bending at the hips, lower your chest to your knees and place your hands on the ground, shoulder-width apart. Jump your legs out behind you to go into a Plank Position (#41), hold it for 2 seconds, and then lower your chest to the ground while keeping your back straight by bending your elbows. Push your torso up until your arms are straight, jump your feet toward your hands, and then jump up into a standing position while reaching overhead. Return to the starting position and repeat this exercise 10 times.

217 Single-Leg Lateral Hops

Tell the children: Start on one leg. Bend the other leg so that your heel is pointing toward your bottom. Begin jumping side to side on only one leg. When you feel fatigue, switch legs. Repeat this whole sequence 5 times.

218 Jump/Jump

Props A box or steps for participants to stand on

Tell the children: Stand on top of a box or a step. Jump forward off of it with both feet. As soon as your feet touch the ground, jump forward as far as you can. Walk back to the step or box and repeat this exercise 10 times.

219 Tuck Jumps

Tell the children: From a standing position, jump up while raising both knees high in front of your body; on the descent, lower your legs slightly and then land softly by keeping your knees bent. Repeat this exercise 10 times.

220 Single-Leg Tuck Jumps

Tell the children: From a standing position, jump up while raising only one knee in front of your body. Lower the knee and land softly. Repeat. When you feel fatigue in one leg, switch legs. Repeat this sequence 5 times.

221 Rectangle Pattern

Tell the children: Standing with your feet together, jump forward 1 time, jump to your right side 2 times, jump backward 1 time, and jump to your left side 2 times. Repeat this sequence 5 times.

222 Somersaults with Jump-Up

Tell the children: Be sure to do this exercise on a mat or soft surface. Start in a standing position and then, bending your knees, perform a somersault. When you finish the somersault, jump up to your feet. Try to add 5 of these to your routine.

223 Sideways

Tell the children: Standing with both legs together, jump to your right side 10 times and then jump to your left side 10 times.

224 Lateral Single-Leg Jumps

Tell the children: Stand on one leg. Bend the other leg so your heel points toward your bottom. Begin jumping side to side with only one leg. Then, as you land, freeze in this position before jumping back to the other side at which point you will freeze again before changing directions. When you feel fatigue, switch legs. Repeat this sequence 5 times.

Variation Jump side to side from one leg to the other, freezing in the landing position on each side before changing directions.

225 Squat-Ups

Tell the children: Stand with your legs together. Bend your knees slightly and then jump up explosively while separating your legs out to the sides of your body. Land softly in a Squat position (#122). Try to add 5 of these to your routine.

226 Jump Shot and Squat

Tell the children: Stand with your feet shoulder-width apart. Get into a Squat position (#122) and place your hands between your knees. Then jump up into a jump-shot position by swinging your arms up over your head. Land softly by bending your knees and return to a squat. Repeat exercise for at least one minute.

227 Split Jumps

Tell the children: Stand with your feet shoulder-width apart. Bend your knees and jump up, swinging your right leg in front of your body and moving your left leg straight behind your body. Let your arms naturally move with your body. Bend your knees to soften your landing and repeat, alternating the front leg. Repeat this sequence 10 times.

228 Traveling Lunge Jumps

Tell the children: Start with your right leg forward in a Backward Lunge (#177) position. Bend both knees and explode upward. As you start to land, move your left leg forward lunge position, dropping your right knee below you. Soften the landing by bending both knees back into a lunge. Repeat this exercise 5 times.

Variation For more of a challenge, have the participants travel this movement forward and backward.

229 Crazy Feet

Tell the children: Imagine a small circle around your body. Begin to jog in place as fast as you can, staying within the circle. Next, move your feet in and out of the imaginary circle as you jog—in an "out-out, in-in" pattern, jogging out to different angles and then back to the center. Pump your arms at your sides. Jog for 1 minute.

230   Distance Jumps

Tell the children: Standing with both feet together, jump as far forward as you can several times in a row. Then jump backward to the starting point and repeat the sequence. Repeat this exercise 5 times.

231   Hopscotch Jumps

Tell the children: Standing with feet together, jump forward with both legs. Then jump forward on only your right leg while raising your left heel toward your bottom. When you land this time, go into a jump with both legs again. Follow this with another single-leg jump forward, this time on your left leg. Repeat this sequence 5 times.

232   Speed Skate

Tell the children: Stand with both of your feet together and your arms at your sides. Jump with both legs to the right, leading slightly with your right leg. Allow your left leg to follow and then cross behind your right foot as it lands, while simultaneously reaching your left arm across your body as if trying to touch the floor. Jump again, this time to the left side. Repeat this sequence 5 times, jumping side to side as quickly as possible.

233   Twists

Tell the children: Stand with your feet a few inches apart. Hop and rotate your knees to the right as you twist your arms to the left, landing with your knees bent. Repeat the sequence, twisting in the opposite direction. Repeat this exercise 5 times.

● ● ● ┊ ● ● ● ┊ ● ● ● ┊ ● ● ● ┊ ● ● ● ┊ ● ● ● ┊ ● ● ● ┊ ● ● ● ┊ ● ● ● ┊ ● ● ● ┊ ● ● ● ┊ ● ● ● ┊ ● ● ● ┊ ● ● ● ┊ ● ● ● ┊ ● ● ●

100   *303 Tween-Approved Exercises and Active Games*

234 Repeated Long Jumps

Tell the children: Stand with your feet together and then jump forward as far as you can. When you land, immediately jump forward again. Make sure to bend your knees to land softly. Repeat this exercise 10 times.

235 Single-Leg Jumps

Tell the children: This movement will be done in a zigzag pattern, so allow for plenty of space. Begin by standing on your right leg with your arms at your sides. Jump diagonally left and land only on your left foot. Immediately jump diagonally forward to the right and land on your right foot. Repeat this exercise 5 times.

236 Squat-Plank-Jump

Tell the children: Squat down with hands touching the ground. Jump back into a Plank Position (#41) with your legs fully extended, your body forming a straight line from your head to your toes, and your arms supporting your body. Jump your legs back into a Squat position (#122). Then jump explosively straight up into the air. Repeat this exercise 5 times.

237 90-Degree Vertical Jumps

Tell the children: Stand with both feet together. Jump explosively upward and, while in the air, turn your body 90 degrees to the side. Repeat this exercise 5 times.

238 180-Degree Vertical Jumps

Tell the children: Stand with both feet together. Jump explosively upward and, while in the air, turn your body 180 degrees so that you face the direction opposite of where you started. Repeat this exercise 5 times.

Sports-Performance Challenges and Drills

Sport Drills are designed to improve athletic performance and reduce risk of injury to the participant. Sport challenges and drills improve core strength and balance, increase power, and enhance the agility and speed needed for every sport. The exercises selected for your tweens in this program simulate movements in speed, biomechanics, and resistance. Safety and proper progression must be a priority. Be sure to read through each drill and practice the movement first without power or speed. Once you have mastered the movement, increase the intensity next.

Start with a Thorough Warm-Up: Have the kids jog 10 minutes at an easy pace and follow it with some simple stretches for their shoulders, hips, ankles, neck, trunk, and head, such as those on pages 24–31. Encourage them to move slowly and breathe deeply.

Maintain Proper Form: Good form means maintaining proper posture while focusing on how you move, not just how fast you move. To ensure proper form, kids should not be fatigued when starting drills. Form is the first thing to suffer when you are tired.

Balance Exercises

Balance training is a fundamental aspect of any training program for overall health and fitness. A strong and flexible core stabilizes your torso and this, along with a good sense of balance, enables you to safely and efficiently stay active and engaged in anything you do, from riding a bike to climbing the stairs. Through a complex system of environmental feedback, cues from the bottom of your feet, the relation of your inner ear to gravity, and what you see, your body senses which muscles to activate or deactivate to maintain your desired position. Explain to the kids that the more they practice balance training, the more quickly and efficiently their bodies will adapt in any specific environment. So proper balance training can reduce the chances of falling and increase the chances of moving correctly while limiting the chance of injury.

239 Book Smart

Props A book for each participant

Before starting this exercise, clear the space of any possible obstacles.

Tell the children: Stand and balance a book on your head for 3 seconds. Then, with the book still on your head and while trying not to drop it, walk backward 10 steps. Turn around and take two small leaps forward, then bend your knees, Squat (#122) as low as you can, and return to the starting position. Continue the exercise for at least 1 minute.

240 Acrobatic Legs

Tell the children: Stand on one leg. Slowly swing the other leg up as high as you can in front of your body and hold it there for 5 seconds. Then slowly swing this same leg behind your body and hold it there for another 5 seconds. Switch legs. Repeat this sequence for at least 1 minute.

241 Tight Rope

Prop Tape or chalk

Place a long piece of tape on the floor or draw a straight line with sidewalk chalk.

Tell the children: Begin by walking the straight line, putting one foot in front of the other. Once this feels easy, jump up as high as you can and try to land perfectly back on the tape or chalk line. Do this exercise 10 times.

242 Wobbly Floor

Tell the children: Stand perfectly still with both feet on the floor together. Now close your eyes, bend your right knee, and bring your knee up in front of you about waist high. Raise your arms out to your sides at shoulder level to help you with balance. Hold this position for 10 seconds and then switch the lead leg. Repeat this sequence for at least 1 minute.

243 V-Sit Challenge

Props A soft ball for each participant

Tell the children: Begin by sitting on the floor with your legs bent and your feet flat on the floor. Place a soft ball between your knees and hold it there by squeezing your inner thighs. Keep your arms off of the floor to challenge your balance. Balancing on your tailbone, slowly straighten out your right leg while keeping your knees in the same place. Slowly straighten your left leg, too, so that both legs are at a 45-degree angle to the floor and your body looks like the letter V.

Grab your legs for support or keep your arms out to your sides for balance. Hold the position for a count of 10 and then return to the starting position. Repeat this exercise for at least 1 minute.

244 Addison Challenge

Tell the children: Begin by sitting on the floor, placing your hands behind your back with your fingers pointing away from your body. Press your feet into the ground and lift your buttocks off the ground. Only your hands and feet should be touching the ground. Lift your right foot off the ground and then lift your left hand off the ground. Try to keep your hips level and hold this position as long as you can. Repeat this movement 5 times and then switch sides.

245 Assisted Lunges

Props A step for each participant

Tell the children: Facing a step, place the ball of your right foot on the edge of the step and keep the ball of your left foot planted on the floor behind you. Keep your arms down at your sides and, placing your weight on your right foot, slowly lower your body, bending your left knee. Then rise back up on your toes and repeat the dip before switching to the other side of your body. Repeat the exercise for at least 1 minute.

246 Rockin' Flexibility

Tell the children: From a standing position, bring your right leg up and out to your right side, keeping it as straight as possible. With your right hand, reach out and try to grab your right toes when you have brought them as high as you can. Hold the position for as long as you can. If you can do it for 15 seconds, you rock! Return to the starting position and switch sides. Repeat the exercise for at least 1 minute.

247 Balance Extensions

Tell the children: Stand tall. Contract your abs and raise your left knee toward your chest, grasping your shin with your hands. Release. Swing the same leg behind you, toes pointed, as you lift that leg, tilt your upper body forward, and extend your arms. Keep your abs tight and your supporting knee slightly bent. Your arms, torso, and extended leg should be aligned. Hold this position for 3 counts. Return to the starting position and switch legs. Repeat the exercise for at least 1 minute.

Variation For a slightly easier exercise, have the participants tap their toes to the floor behind them instead of lifting their leg.

The following series of drills are intended to improve visual tracking, hand–eye coordination, agility, speed, visual tracking, and listening skills. These drills will improve your tweens' performance in all sports.

248 Mirror Image

This is a fun game, and it is a wonderful way to improve response time and co-ordination skills. Divide the group into pairs or have the players choose partners.

Tell the children: One person is "It." This person performs a sports movement and travels the movement around a space. The other player must copy every action and stay face-to-face with his partner. Perform 5 movements with your partner and then switch roles.

249 Racquet Skills

Props A tennis racquet and ball for each participant

Tell the children: Holding the racquet in front of your body, count the number of times you can keep a tennis ball bouncing on the strings of your racquet without it hitting the floor. If you drop the ball, you must start counting from zero again. Play 5 rounds.

250 Dribble the Ball

Props A tennis racquet and ball for each participant

Tell the children: Using the racquet, dribble the tennis ball in place. Once you have mastered the drill, you can add travel movements. For example, you can walk forward and dribble, walk backward and dribble, shuffle side to side and dribble, and run and dribble. How many times in a row can you bounce the tennis ball? Play 5 rounds.

251 Flipping

Props A tennis racquet and ball for each participant

Tell the children: Using the racquet and ball, bounce the ball on the strings of the racquet. When you have mastered this movement, flip the racquet over each time you hit the ball. Count the number of times you can bounce the ball on alternating sides of the racquet without letting the ball fall to the floor. Play 5 rounds.

Foot Drills

One thing that all sports have in common is footwork. Foot drills will help improve speed, coordination, recovery, and strength. Get creative with your drills by creating shapes, patterns, or even alphabet letters for footwork. For footwork drills, you will need cones, markers, and balls. You can purchase these in a sporting-goods store.

252 All Out

Props A series of cones for each pair

Set up a series of 3 cones or markers about 10 feet apart in a straight line. Divide the group into pairs or have the players choose partners.

Tell the children: One player starts as a "runner," and the other partner plays the role of "caller." The runner starts by sitting cross-legged near the middle cone. When you, as the caller, say "Go," your partner stands up and runs to the right cone. From there, he turns around, runs backward to the middle cone, and sits down cross-legged again. You may call out the right cone, the left cone, or either cone, and your partner must run forward to that cone, backward back to the middle cone, and sit down again. Repeat this exercise for 3 to 5 minutes and then switch roles.

253 Have a Ball

Props A series of cones and a ball for each pair

Set up a series of 3 cones or markers about 10 feet apart in a straight line. Divide the group into pairs or have the players choose partners.

Tell the children: One player starts as the "runner," and the other partner plays the role of "caller." The running partner starts by sitting down cross-legged in the middle of the cones. The caller says "Go," and tells the runner which direction to run. As the runner runs, the caller may shout, "Ball" and throw a ball to the runner. The runner must catch the ball and immediately throw it back to the caller. The caller can throw the ball or tell the runner to change directions at any time. Repeat this exercise for 3 to 5 minutes and then switch roles.

254 Sprint/Sidestep

Props A series of cones

Set up a series of cones or markers approximately 25 feet apart in a straight line.

Tell the children: The object of this drill is to coordinate two different styles of movement. Players will alternate by sprinting to one cone and sidestepping to the next cone. Line up by the first cone. One player will be the "Caller." When he says, "Go," everyone sprints to the first cone. When you reach it, turn and sidestep to the next cone. Then sprint back to the middle cone and sidestep back to starting position. Play the game for 5 minutes and then choose a new player to become the caller.

255　Shuttle Run

Props Cones or other markers

Tell the children: The shuttle run is a standard agility and speed drill used by athletes who play stop-and-go sports such as soccer, hockey, basketball, and tennis. Set up two markers about 25 yards apart. Sprint from one marker to the other and back. That's one repetition. Do 5 repetitions.

Variations There are a variety of different ways to do the shuttle run, including side-to-side runs, forward-backward runs, and forward-touch-return runs (in which players touch the marker before returning). The shuttle run is an easy way to add some high-intensity drills to a basic exercise program while you build speed, stamina, and endurance.

256　Run and Catch

Props A ball for each pair

This is a popular football drill. Divide the group into pairs or have the players choose partners.

　Tell the children: Choose one partner to be the runner and one to be the thrower. The runner runs about 25 steps and turns. The thrower then throws the ball to the runner, who catches it. The runner returns to the starting position and, the next time out, runs a zigzag pattern before turning to catch the ball. Complete 5 plays and then switch roles.

> ### Exercises to improve stride length and frequency include:
>
> - Speed Skate (#232)
> - Hurdle Jumping (#257)
> - Single-Leg Lateral Hops (#217)
> - Run in Place with High Knees (#196)
> - running in a swimming pool
> - Side Skip-Ups (#214)
> - Jumping Rope (#288)

257 Hurdle Jumping

Props Hurdles or small objects to mark the places where participants should jump

Place hurdles about 3 to 4 feet apart, staggering them so they are not in a straight line. Include as many hurdles around your space as possible. If you don't have hurdles, use small objects to mark spots for the kids to jump.

Tell the children: Jumping over hurdles increases your rebound quickness, allowing you to jump off the ground more quickly and with coordination. Begin by running and jumping with both feet over each hurdle. Then, on your second round around the course, run sideways and jump over each hurdle. Do 5 laps.

258 Clock Pattern

This game challenges the coordination, speed, and accuracy of the player.

Tell the children: Starting as if you are standing in the middle of an imaginary clock, jump both feet out to a twelve o'clock position and immediately jump back to the middle. Next, jump to one o'clock and back to middle. Jump to each of the hours of a clock, always jumping back to the center before jumping out to a new hour. Do 5 repetitions of the clock pattern.

259 Speed Drills

Prop A stopwatch or clock

Tell the children: To increase your speed in running, you need to improve the power and strength in your legs. Designate a start line and a finish line. Start your stopwatch and run forward as fast as you can from start to finish. Record your time and repeat the exercise 10 times.

260 Sprints

Interval running involves short bursts of running at maximum speed. Each interval should be 6 to 8 seconds long, with a full recovery period in between.

Tell the children: Try sprints with side shuffles, Skipping (#206), and running backward.

Here is an example of an interval run:

- 1 to 5 minutes light to medium jog
- 2 minutes maximum run
- 6 seconds maximum speed
- 2 minutes medium jog
- 8 seconds maximum run
- 2 minutes medium jog
- 8 seconds maximum run
- 1 minute medium jog
- 8 seconds maximum run
- 2 minutes medium jog
- 6 seconds maximum run
- 2 minutes medium to light jog

Total: Approximately 15 minutes of interval training.
Double this workout pattern for a 30-minute workout.

261 Resistance Running

Divide the group into pairs or have the players choose partners.

Tell the children: Resisted sprints involve dragging some form of resistance behind you as you run. You can also perform this with a resistance band or a long jump rope around your waist, held by a partner. Run for 3 minutes.

Variation Sprint uphill in a park or on hiking trails, on a treadmill, or in sand.

Coordination and Agility

Balance, rhythm, spatial orientation, and the ability to react to both auditory and visual stimuli have all been identified as elements of coordination. In fact, the development of good coordination is a multi-tiered sequence that progresses from skills performed with good spatial awareness but without speed to skills performed at increased speeds and in a constantly changing environment. Coordination is best developed between the ages of 7 and 13, with the most crucial period being between 10 and 13 years of age.

Agility is the ability to explosively stop, change direction, and accelerate again. Sports such as tennis, baseball, basketball, football, soccer, softball, and volleyball require athletes to be agile. Therefore, since all of these are popular youth sports, kids should work to improve their agility. Quality is the key for successful performance of these speed-and-agility drills. Keep the individual sprints short and have the kids rest between sets.

262   Coordination Challenge

Tell the children: You must listen carefully and watch carefully to fully succeed in this challenge. The leader will say and perform a movement, and you have to perform the complete opposite. Some examples are:

- If the leader runs forward, the player must run backward.
- If the leader hops on left leg, the player must hop on right leg.
- If the leader circles right arm, the player must circle left arm.
- If the leader sidesteps right, the player must sidestep left.
- If the leader does a forward somersault, the player must do a backward somersault.

263   Jump-Overs

Prop A jump rope or tape measure approximately 6 to 10 feet long or chalk

Use a jump rope, tape measure, or chalk to create a straight line on the floor.

Tell the children: Stand at one end of the line, facing the length of the rope with both feet together. Jump from one side of the line to the other, keeping both feet together and traveling forward for the full length of the line. Then jump from one side of the line to the other for the full length of the line, traveling backward. Repeat this exercise 5 times.

264   Run-Overs

Prop A jump rope

Tell the children: Stand at one end, facing the length of the rope that is stretched out on the ground. Travel forward, running over the rope without touching it and crossing over it with each step. To do this, face the length of the jump rope and cross your right foot over to the left side of the rope without touching it; then immediately cross your left foot over to the right side of the rope. When you reach the end of the rope, run the length of it traveling backward. Repeat this entire sequence 10 times.

265   Crisscross, Straddle Jumps

Prop A jump rope

Tell the children: Stand at the end of the rope that is stretched out on the ground, facing the length of it. Jump up and crisscross your legs before you land with a foot on each side of the rope. For example:

Jump up and land with your right foot on the left side of the rope and your left foot on the right side of the rope. Next, jump up and straddle the rope with your right foot on the right side of rope and your left foot on the left side of the rope. Alternate between criss-cross and straddle jumps. When you reach the end of the rope, turn around and repeat the sequence. Jump for 1 minute.

266   Little Jumps

Prop A jump rope

Tell the children: Facing the width of a rope stretched out on the ground and with your toes almost touching it, jump forward and backward over the rope, traveling sideways up the length of the rope. Once you reach one end of the rope, travel in the opposite direction, continuing to jump forward and backward. Complete this sequence 5 times.

267   Kick It

Tell the children: Begin by leading with your right leg into a Backward Lunge (#177) position. Push up and forward with your right leg while your left leg kicks forward. Immediately return to a backward lunge and start the entire sequence over. Repeat this exercise 10 times before switching legs.

268　Fast Hip Rotations

Tell the children: Stand with your feet hip-width apart and then, while staying on the balls of your feet, jump up and forward while rotating your hips so the right one is forward. Immediately jump up and rotate 180 degrees so your left hip is now facing forward. Each time you jump you will be jumping forward, so by the time you finish 10 hip rotations you should be at least 5 feet away from where you started. After doing this 10 times, turn around and repeat until you are back in the starting position. Be sure to increase your speed as you repeat. Repeat the exercise for at least 1 minute.

269　Agility Challenge: Running

Divide the group into pairs or have the players choose partners.

Tell the children: One partner is the leader for this game. The leader begins running in one direction and then, without warning, quickly changes direction. The other partner must follow the leader, watching for any changes of direction she makes. This game focuses on visual training for agility. Continue running for 1 minute before switching roles.

270　High-Knees Running

Tell the children: As you begin to run, lift your knees waist high as you run. Run this way for 1 minute.

271　Army Crawl

Tell the children: Lie on the floor facedown, with your arms overhead. Bend your right knee out and, keeping it against the floor, move it up toward your right hand, pushing against your knee to travel forward. Immediately bring your left knee up toward your left arm and continue moving forward. You will look like an alligator when performing this move. Crawl for 1 or 2 minutes.

Variation Backward crawl. We can all crawl forward, but it takes even greater coordination to crawl backward.

272 Agility Challenge: Personal Best

Props A clock or stopwatch; 2 cones or markers

Set the two cones 25 feet apart.

Tell the children: This is a timed game. Starting at one cone, run as fast as you can to the other cone, tap it, and then run back to the starting position. Check your time and try to beat your own personal best record. To make this more challenging, set the cones farther apart. Each player takes 5 runs.

273 Linear Speed and Agility

Props Two cones or other markers

Place the cones or markers 25 feet apart.

Tell the children: Starting from one cone, travel laterally, doing Shuffle Steps (#189) sideways. When you reach the other cone, touch it and shuffle back to the starting point. Repeat this exercise 5 times.

274 The Big Weave

Props Four cones or markers

Place four cones or markers in a line with each 10 feet apart.

Tell the children: Run forward and weave between the cones, always facing forward. When you get to the last cone, turn around and repeat the action, returning to the starting point. Repeat this exercise 5 times.

275 Bear Run

Tell the children: With your weight on your hands and feet, walk forward 10 steps, backward 10 steps, sideways 10 steps, and then sideways 10 steps to the other side. Repeat this sequence 5 times.

276 Agility Challenge: Moving Sideways

Divide the group into pairs or have the players choose partners.

Tell the children: One partner is the "caller." When the caller shouts, "Go," the other partner runs sideways; when the caller yells, "Change," the partner switches direction and runs sideways back to the starting position. The caller can change the direction many times. Continue for 1 minute and then switch roles.

277 Agility Challenge: Running Straight

Divide the group into pairs or have the players choose partners.

Tell the children: Identify a start line and one partner to be the "caller." When the caller says, "Go," the other player runs forward as fast as he can. When the caller says, "Switch," the player must turn around and run back to the starting line. The caller can change direction many times. Continue for 1 minute and then switch roles.

278 Agility Challenge: Sidesteps

Divide the group into pairs or have the players choose partners.

Tell the children: Stand with your feet hip-width apart. When your partner says, "Go," begin a sidestep movement by bending your knees slightly and taking a large step sideways. If you are traveling to your right, your right foot steps to the side followed by your left foot coming to meet your right foot. Continue taking large sidesteps until your partner says, "Switch." Then you must change the direction of your sidestep and move in the opposite directions. Continue for 1 minute and then switch roles.

279 Lift and Kick

Tell the children: Lift your right leg in front of you, bending your knee at a 90-degree angle. Your thigh should be parallel to the floor. Sweep your leg back, pressing through the heel. Without touching the floor, lift your leg up in front again and repeat. Repeat the exercise for at least 1 minute and then switch legs.

280　Heel Walk/Toe Walk

Tell the children: With your feet flexed and your toes pointed toward the ceiling, walk for 30 seconds on your heels. Try moving this way for at least 1 minute. Then walk on the balls of your feet with your heels off the floor for 30 seconds. Repeat this whole sequence for at least 1 minute.

281　Step Knee-Ups

Tell the children: From a standing position, step forward with your right leg. Immediately swing your left knee up in front of your body. Lower your knee and repeat the movement several times with the same knee before switching lead legs. This movement only travels forward. Repeat the exercise for at least 1 minute.

282　Stair Running

Prop A flight of stairs

Tell the children: Taking turns, run up and walk down the stairs. Repeat this exercise for at least 1 minute, running as many flights of stairs as you can.

283　Every Other Step

Prop A flight of stairs

Tell the children: Climb a flight of stairs, taking two steps at a time. Do not use speed on this movement and be sure to walk down the steps one at a time. Repeat this exercise for at least 1 minute, climbing as many flights of stairs as you can.

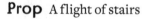

284 Lunges with Lift

Prop A flight of stairs

Tell the children: Stand facing the stairs, standing on your left leg. Standing Lunge (#127) forward, placing your right leg on top of one of the steps. Be sure to bend both knees and avoid extending the right knee past your toes on your right foot. Push straight up with your right leg until you are on the toes of your right foot. Slowly lower yourself back into the starting position and switch legs. Repeat for 1 minute.

285 Incline Step Sit-Ups

Props A mat or towel for each participant; a flight of stairs

Tell the children: Lie down in front of the steps with your feet facing them. You may want to put a mat or a towel down for a cushion. Place both feet flat on the second or third step. Interlace your fingers behind your head. Keeping your lower back pressed against the floor, curl up your spine and upper body into a sit-up position and then slowly roll back down into the starting position. Repeat the exercise for at least 1 minute.

286 Agility Challenge: Throwing a Ball

Props A small ball for each pair

Divide the group into pairs or have the players choose partners.

    Tell the children: Stand 15 feet away from your partner but face each other. Begin to throw a ball back and forth. Then your partner will begin to move sideways; you must move with her. So if your partner slides to her left, you must slide to your right while continually throwing the ball back and forth. Continue moving and throwing the ball for 1 minute.

287 One-Arm Throws

Props A ball for each pair

Divide the group into pairs or have the players choose partners.

    Tell the children: Stand about 25 feet away from your partner.

Pick up a small- to medium-size ball in one hand and throw it to your partner. Your partner must also catch and throw the ball with one hand. Repeat this sequence 5 times.

288 Jumping Rope

Props A jump rope for each participant

Tell the children: In a standing position, hold your elbows at your sides and turn the rope smoothly with your wrists. Take one jump per revolution, and keep your feet close to the floor when you jump. Work up to 20 minutes or more of jumping.

Variations

- Both feet: As the rope circles around your body, jump up high with both feet.

- One foot only: As the rope circles around your body, jump over the rope using one leg the entire time. After 1 minute, switch legs.

- Alternate feet: As the rope circles around your body, jump over the rope using one leg at a time and alternating legs between jumps.

- Scissor jumps: As the rope circles around your body, jump over the rope with the right leg in front and the left leg back. As you jump, switch leg positions.

- Intervals of speed: Increase and decrease the speed at which the rope cycles. Try thirty-second intervals of speed jumping. Then slow down the speed of the rope and do thirty seconds of slow jumping using any variation of foot patterns.

- Can-can jump: As the rope circles around your body, bring your right knee up in front of you for the first rotation. On the next jump rope rotation, return your right foot to the floor and immediately bring your right foot forward and up into a full kick. Repeat with left foot: one knee up, touch down, and full kick. Continue switching legs after each kick.

- Jumping-jack skier: As the rope circles around your body, jump over the rope keeping feet together. Jump side to side with your legs together.

Get Your Game On!

Exercise comes in all shapes and forms. Not all kids like sports, but most will join in on fun games, especially when friends, family, and a little friendly competition are involved. Remember exercise does not have to mean a boring set of push-ups or sit-ups—exercise can be in a game of tag or a relay race, it is an activity in its own right and this is a relatively new concept. Moving is the key, playing, being active. When kids begin to see that physical activity is not a chore, but as worthwhile exciting activities, they will play.

Play is soul charging—it allows us to let problems and stress go and be totally serious about fun.

289 Capture the Flag

whole group

Props Two goals; 2 flags

You need at least 6 players for this game. Divide the players into teams.

Tell the children: The object of the game is to capture the other team's flag without being tagged and bring it back safely to your home base. To begin the game, each team must place their flag somewhere within their territory and identify a "jail." When a player is tagged, he must head to jail until either the game is over or a teammate sneaks over to the jail to untag him and release him from jail. On the word "Go" from the leader, players can cross over to steal the flag or stay behind to protect their own flag. The game is won when a player returns to his own territory with the enemy's flag without getting caught.

290   H-O-R-S-E

Props   A basketball hoop; a basketball

You need 2 or more players for this game.

Tell the children: To begin the game, the first player shoots the ball from anywhere on the court. If she makes the shot, then the next player must copy the same shot from the same position on the court. If he misses, he receives the first letter "h," and the next player must make the original shot. However, if the second player makes the shot, he receives no letter, he now takes a shot from anywhere on the court, and the game continues. The first player to receive all letters in the word horse loses.

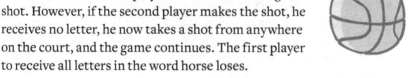

291   Around the World

Props   A basketball hoop; a basketball

You need at least 2 players for this game.

Tell the children: The object of the game is to shoot from various positions around the hoop. Choose a spot on the court that is fairly close to the hoop; this is the position from which everyone must begin shooting. Shooting straight on is the 0 mark; moving to the side makes the next marks at 30, 60, and 90 degrees. Making a basket from a position allows a player to advance to the next position. A player keeps advancing around the world until he misses, and then the other player(s) get a chance. To win the game, a player must make a basket from all of the designated positions.

292   Twenty-One

Props   A basketball hoop; a basketball

You need at least 2 players for this game.

Tell the children: In this basketball game, each player keeps her own score. The game begins with the first player to make a basket. The player shoots the ball and tries to rebound the ball to shoot again. The other players can attempt to stop the score by defending the hoop. No one has teammates; it's every player for herself. The player with the ball may shoot at anytime and rebound and shoot again. The first player to collect 21 points is the winner.

293 Dodgeball

Props A collection of large, soft balls

Divide the players into 2 teams.

Tell the children: Using a large, soft ball, throw the ball below the waist of a player from the opposite team. If you hit this player without him catching the ball, he is out. If he catches the ball you threw at him, you are out. The team with the last remaining player wins.

294 Blanket Ball

Props Two beach towels; 1 ball

Divide the players into two teams. Place the blankets at each end of the field and put the ball in the middle. Set a duration for the game before starting.

Tell the children: The objective of the game is to get the ball onto the other team's goal, which is a blanket. Players can pass or kick the ball toward their opponents' goal, but when they are in possession of the ball, they can be tagged by the other team and must freeze in place until a team scores a goal, in which case everyone is unfrozen. And when a team scores a goal, all players return to their base, and the team that lost the point starts with the ball. When time runs out, the team with the most points wins.

295 Shaving Cream Fight

Props Nonmenthol shaving cream for each participant; a water hose for cleaning up after the game

This game is fun and great for parties. There isn't a winner or loser in this game; it's just a blast.

Tell the children: Each player gets a can of shaving cream. On the word "Go," each player tries to cream another player.

296 Four Square

Prop A standard red kickball

For the standard game, mark 4 squares on the ground, all touching each other and making 1 larger square. Each small square is roughly 8' × 8', but that's not a hard-and-fast rule. The ball used is the standard red "kickball."

Tell the children: Each of the first 4 players occupies 1 of the squares. The squares each have a numbered rank order from 1 to 4. The square with the highest rank is called the "king" or "queen." The other squares sometimes have names and sometime don't.

The king serves the ball by bouncing it into one of the other squares. The receiving player then hits the ball into any other player's square and play continues until one of the following things occurs:

1. a player hits the ball (or is hit BY the ball) before it bounces once in her square

2. a player does not hit the ball before it bounces twice

3. a player hits the ball out of bounds (it must land in someone's square first)

Once a player is "dead," the other players move up to fill the vacancy, and she moves back to the lowest-ranking square or gets in line behind other tweens who are waiting to get into the game.

297 Chinese Jump Rope

Props A Chinese jump rope for each group of three

You will need a Chinese jump rope to play this game. You can buy them at toy stores or sporting-goods stores.

Tell the children: Begin with the rope around the ankles of 2 players.

Another player jumps inside the rope with both feet. Then he jumps out of the rope with both legs straddling each outside rope. Next, the player jumps on both ropes and then jumps from side to side, taking turns straddling each side of the rope. Then the player jumps on the rope and out again. Finally, the player crosses the rope, using his legs, so that his legs are inside of an x. With that he jumps out and lands, straddling the rope.

With each jump, the player must land where he means to land. If the player lands on the rope when he is not supposed to or if he is trying to land on the rope and misses, then his turn is over. Once a player accomplishes the ankles, he moves up to the waist, then below the arms, and then finally the neck. (I have never seen it go that far.) With each sequence, the players say, "In, out, side, side, on, in, out."

Variation The player jumps inside the rope, then outside the rope and jumps on to the rope. Finally, the player jumps out of the rope and crosses the rope, using his legs, so that his legs are inside of an x. With that he jumps out and lands, straddling the rope.

298 The Blob

You need at least 6 players for this game.

Tell the children: Two people start the game by being "The Blob." They hold hands and chase the other players. If a player is caught, that person joins "the Blob" by linking hands with players in the existing Blob. The more players that the Blob catches, the bigger it grows. The Blob can decide if it wants to split in two if it grows too big. The game is done when everyone has been captured.

299 Skyball

Props One lightweight ball; a garage or other short building that you can throw a ball over and run all the way around

You need at least 6 players for this game. Divide the group into 2 teams.

Tell the children: One group is the throwing and running team; the other team is the catching and tagging team. The teams stand on opposite sides of the building.

The game begins by one team calling out "Skyball!" and throwing the ball over the garage to the kids on the other side. The second group must catch the ball, sneak around the building, and throw the ball at their opponents or tag them with it. The "throwers" must keep an eye open for the "catchers" coming around the building, and they must run to the opposite side from which they threw the ball to be safe. If a player makes it to the opposite side, then that becomes his side, but any player who are tagged become part of the opposing team. When a team includes more than 3 or 4 kids, the team can split up, with some members going each way. Then the throwers won't know who has the ball.

If the ball is not caught, then the catchers can wait a moment to try to fool you, yell "Skyball!" and throw the ball back. If the ball doesn't go over the building, the throwers then try to throw it again. Catchers must catch the ball in order to run around the building after their opponents. When the last kid on a team is tagged, the game is over.

300 Footballoon

Props Water balloons

This is the ideal football drill to conclude practice on a hot summer day. Coaches and assistants line up beside players and toss water balloons at them as they run through the ladder drill. Players are motivated to be particularly quick and agile to stay in the game.

Tell the children: As you run through the ladder drill, your coaches and their assistants will toss water balloons at you. Once you have been hit, you are out. The last player remaining wins and might get the reward of tossing a few balloons at the coach.

301 Three-Legged Race

Props A scarf or ribbon for each pair

Assign partners. Be sure to match size and skill level. Designate a start line and a finish line.

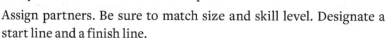

Tell the children: Stand next to your partner and put your arm around your partner's waist. Tie your inside leg together with your partner's inside leg. On "Go," walk with your partner as fast as you can to the finish line. Whichever pair finishes first wins.

302 Floppy Socks

Props Enough socks for each participant to have a pair to wear

Tell the children: The object of the game is to collect as many socks as you can from other players. Pull your socks down and off your feet a bit so they are flopping and hanging off. On "Go," crawl around the floor, trying to steal other players' socks while protecting your own. When all of the socks have been removed, the player with the most socks wins.

303 Suicides

Props Five pieces of tape in 5-foot lengths; a stopwatch

Make five parallel lines about 2 yards, 3 yards, 4 yards, and 5 yards apart.

Tell the children: Each player will run from the first line to the second line and then run back to the start. Next, players run from the first line to the third line and run back. They then run from the first line to the fourth line and then back to the start.

Finally, they run from the first line to the fifth line and back. Each time a player gets to a line, she must touch it with both hands. Use a stopwatch to record each player's time. The object of this game is to finish the course the fastest.

Variation For more of a challenge, have participants do 1 or more Push-Ups (#102) when they get to each line.

Circuit Station/ Interval Training

Total-body circuit training involves muscle strengthening and cardiovascular training because you are quickly moving through each circuit of exercises. Circuit stations create muscle confusion by using one group of muscles and quickly moving on to another group of muscles. Have the kids perform each station for 1 minute, move quickly from one exercise to the next, and repeat the entire total body circuit 5 to 10 times. You can have them use the sample circuit stations below or create a circuit of your own together.

Station: Over the Top

- warm-up: slow dancing
- Chest Stretch (#3)
- Side Stretch (#4)
- Star Pose (#29)
- Roll-Backs (#42)
- Windmills (#53)
- Wall Squats (#154)
- Squat Jumping Jacks (#211)
- Run-Overs (#264)

Station: Baseball

- run in place
- Triangle Pose (#33)
- Abdominal Crunches (#75)
- Crisscross Reverse Flies (#93)
- Push-Ups (#102)
- Squats (#122)
- Standing Lunges (#127)
- Jump Shot and Squat (#226)
- Twists (#233)

Station: Basketball

- Mountain Pose (#28)
- Warrior Pose (#31)
- Wall Squats (#154)
- Plank with Arm Circle (#180)
- Squat Jumping Jacks (#211)
- Rebound Running (#212)
- Tuck Jumps (#219)
- 180-Degree Vertical Jumps (#238)
- V-Sit Challenge (#243)
- Jumping Rope (#288)

Station: Dance

- Tree Pose (#32)
- Downward-Facing Dog (#34)
- The Hundreds (#37)
- Charleston (#183)
- Figure 8s (#185)
- Shuffle Steps (#189)

- Step/Kicks (#190)
- Toe-Touch Kicks (#192)
- Heel-to-Bottom Jumps (#193)
- Pony (#198)

Station: Mind and Body

- Cow Pose (#20)
- Cobra (#21)
- Front-Lying Boat Pose (#23)
- Tabletop (#24)
- Half Locust Pose (#25)
- Crescent Moon Pose (#30)
- Warrior Pose (#31)
- Downward-Facing Dog (#34)
- Chair Pose (#35)
- Standing Twists (#36)

Station: Soccer

- Plank Position (#41)
- Swimming (#45)
- Windmills (#53)
- Seesaw (#78)
- Push-Ups (#102)
- Front Kicks (#120)
- Squats (#122)
- Squat Jumping Jacks (#211)
- Run and Catch (#256)

Station: Skateboarding

- Cobra (#21)
- Downward-Facing Dog (#34)
- Roll-Backs (#42)
- V Sit-Ups (#66)
- Side Plank (#81)
- Vertical Depth Jumps (#208)
- Rebound Running (#212)
- Tuck Jumps (#219)
- Split Jumps (#227)
- 90-Degree Vertical Jumps (#237)

Station: Skiing

- Push-Ups (#102)
- Squats (#122)
- Bottom Blaster (#131)
- Wall Squats (#154)
- Run in Place with High Knees (#196)
- Vertical Depth Jumps (#208)
- Squat Jumping Jacks (#211)
- Speed Skate (#232)
- Jump-Overs (#263)
- Incline Step Sit-Ups (#285)

Station: Flexibility

- Cobra (#21)
- Tabletop (#24)
- Mountain Pose (#28)
- Star Pose (#29)
- Chair Pose (#35)
- Scissors (#39)
- Rear-Leg Kickbacks (#40)
- Roll-Backs (#42)
- Breaststroke (#47)
- Full-Body Roll-Ups (#48)

Station: Heart Pumping

- Overhead Throws (#203)
- Skipping (#206)
- Advanced Mountain Climber with Speed (#207)
- Leaping (#210)
- Squat Jumping Jacks (#211)
- Rebound Running (#212)
- Power Jump-Ups (#215)
- Squat-Thrust-Jump Rocket (#216)
- Jump/Jump (#218)
- Speed Skate (#232)

Station: Swimming

- Roll-Backs (#42)
- Swimming (#45)
- Breaststroke (#47)
- Spine Stretch (#49)
- Knee Circles (#50)
- Windmills (#53)
- Abdominal Crunches (#75)
- Pointer Reaches (#76)
- Side Plank (#81)
- Squats (#122)

Station: Football

- Triceps Challenge (#95)
- Biceps Curls (#96)
- Push-Ups (#102)
- Squats (#122)
- Standing Lunges (#127)
- Squat Pulses (#149)
- Wall Slides (#153)
- Squat Jumping Jacks (#211)
- Tuck Jumps (#219)
- Clock Pattern (#258)

Station: Killer Camp

- Plank Position (#41)
- Triceps Challenge (#95)
- Push-Ups (#102)
- Plank with Single-Knee Lift (#148)
- Jumping Jacks (#163)
- Forward Lunges with Biceps Curl (#172)
- Squat Jumping Jacks (#211)
- Single-Leg Tuck Jumps (#220)
- Squat-Ups (#225)

Station: Core Challenge

- Cobra (#21)
- Tabletop (#24)
- Swimming (#45)
- Windmills (#53)
- Ball Twists (#55)
- Crunches with Knee Rolls (#58)
- Can-Opener Crunches (#65)
- Bicycle (#71)
- Pointer Reaches (#76)
- Side Plank (#81)

Station: Martial Arts

- Double-Leg Lifts (#74)
- Lower-Back Strengthener (#80)
- Supreme Fold (#86)
- Triceps Dips (#116)
- Forward Jabs (#117)
- Cross Jabs (#118)
- Front Kicks (#120)
- Roundhouse Kicks (#121)
- Squats (#122)
- Tuck Jumps (#219)

Station: Running

- Squats (#122)
- Leg Circles (#158)
- Walking Lunges (#182)
- Toe-Touch Kicks (#192)
- Skater Lunges (#202)
- Skipping (#206)
- Leaping (#210)
- Rebound Running (#212)
- 180-Degree Vertical Jumps (#238)
- Jumping Rope (#288)

Station: Hiking

- V Sit-Ups (#66)
- Double-Leg Lifts (#74)
- Seesaw (#78)
- Mountain Climber (#138)
- Figure-4 Squats (#139)
- Squat Pulses (#149)
- Jogging (#194)
- Skipping (#206)
- Squat Jumping Jacks (#211)
- Side Skip-Ups (#214)

Station: Tennis

- Windmills (#53)
- Walking Lunges (#182)
- Side Throws (#204)
- Skipping (#206)
- Advanced Mountain Climber with Speed (#207)
- Squat Jumping Jacks (#211)
- Mirror Image (#248)
- Racquet Skills (#249)
- Flipping (#251)
- Have a Ball (#253)
- Agility Challenge: Running (#269)
- Army Crawl (#271)

Station: Golf

- Downward-Facing Dog (#34)
- Scissors (#39)
- V Sit-Ups (#66)
- Side Plank (#81)
- External Rotations (#114)
- One-Legged Squats (#136)
- Run in Place with High Knees (#196)
- Squat Jumping Jacks (#211)
- Twists (#233)
- One-Arm Throws (#287)

Station: Cycling

- Scissors (#39)
- Rolling Like a Ball (#44)
- Spine Stretch (#49)
- Bicycle (#71)
- Seesaw (#78)
- Crisscross Reverse Flies (#93)
- Contract and Extend (#132)
- Heel Lifts (#152)
- Wall Squats (#154)

Station: Military

- Forearm-Plank Knee Touches (#72)
- Abdominal Crunches (#75)
- Biceps Curls (#96)
- Push-Ups (#102)
- Triceps Dips (#116)
- Front Kicks (#120)
- Roundhouse Kicks (#121)
- Run in Place with High Knees (#196)
- Squat Jumping Jacks (#211)
- Rebound Running (#212)

Station: Morning Workout

- Cow Pose (#20)
- Cobra (#21)
- Tabletop (#24)
- Mountain Pose (#28)
- Warrior Pose (#31)
- Triangle Pose (#33)
- Bicycle (#71)
- Push and Touch (#91)
- Push-Ups (#102)
- Squat Jumping Jacks (#211)

Station: Bedtime Workout

- Cow Pose (#20)
- Cobra (#21)
- Star Pose (#29)
- Tree Pose (#32)
- Tilt and Lift (#38)
- Rolling Like a Ball (#44)
- Reverse Roll-Downs (#46)
- Breaststroke (#47)
- Spine Stretch (#49)
- Knee Circles (#50)

Outdoor Challenges

Exercise is great for your body and your state of mind. Exercising outdoors can boost self-esteem and mood. Let the world be your gym with the following fun family fitness adventures.

Outdoor Challenge

- Warm up: Jog with knees high and hands clapping under your alternating knees for 1 minute.
- Walk for 1 minute.
- Do 1 minute of Step/Kicks (#190).
- Do 1 minute of Bear Run (#275).
- Do 1 minute of Skipping (#206).
- Do 1 minute of Jumping Rope (#288).
- Do the Plank Position (#41).
- Do 10 Triceps Dips (#116).
- Do 10 Mountain Climbers (#138).
- Swim 4 laps in a pool.
- Bike 3 miles.
- Bike 2.5 miles.
- Run 1 mile.
- Stretch to cool down.
- Do Cow Pose (#20).
- Do Cobra (#21).
- Do Mountain Pose (#28).

Bird Walk

Bring binoculars and field guides if you have them and learn what to watch for in habits, physical characteristics, and calls. The walk should take about 3 hours. This is a great physical activity for all ages. Recommend that any participants wear long pants and closed-toe shoes and bring along sunscreen, insect repellent, and water. Google search your local parks for information on native birds.

Geocaching

Searching for treasure! Go to www.geocaching.com and search for geocaching in your local area. If you don't have a local geocaching organization, start one in your local park. Geocaching is a sort of GPS-powered treasure hunt, and according to a new study it may hold the key to getting kids and family members to exercise.

Orienteering

Orienteering is a fun form of land navigation for the entire family. This sport started out as a form of military training in the nineteenth century and has become a popular sport for everyone. To play, all you need are a compass and a detailed map to find points in the landscape. Orienteering can be enjoyed as a walk in the woods that allows you to learn how to use a compass or it can be done as a professional sport, in which case it is a timed event.

A standard orienteering course consists of a starting area and a series of points, called control sites or clues, which are designated on a map. By following the symbols on the map, you try to find each clue. When you find a clue, you verify your visit by using a hole punch hanging next to the flag to mark your control card. Follow all the clues and head for the finish line. Many different types of orienteering exist; for example, you can navigate by foot, mountain bike, ski, and canoe. You can play an orienteering game by planning a route on a map and then timing the route. It's a great way to learn new skills, enjoy nature, burn calories, and have a good time with your family and friends.

Trail Adventure

Introduce the idea of respecting the environment when participating in outdoor activities. Environmental awareness is a social issue, and children should be encouraged early to learn about environmental conservation and preservation. They could be told that everyone has an impact on their surroundings and that our natural resources are valuable and limited so it's up to us to respect and conserve them.

It is important to teach kids to develop a sense of stewardship for the natural world, to understand how to be safe and prepared for adventures in the outdoors and to understand how to reduce impact on the environment when recreating outdoors.

The PEAK (Promoting Environmental Awareness in Kids) program is the result of a unique partnership between REI (Recreation Equipment, Inc.) and the Leave No Trace Center for Outdoor Ethics. PEAK is based on the seven principles of Leave No Trace and is designed to educate children about the outdoors and the responsible use of our shared public lands. For more information, call (800) 332-4100 or e-mail info@lnt.org. To learn more about environmental awareness and Leave No Trace visit http://lnt.org/learn/7-principles.

Let the World Be Your Gym

Are you inspired by the outdoors? Explore it and all it has to offer. Instead of running on a treadmill, try one of the following outdoor activities:

- walking
- 5k challenge
- cycling
- running
- power walking
- hiking
- swimming

Water Works

Exercising in the pool is a great way to burn calories, tone your muscles, and have fun all at the same time. The buoyancy of water reduces the "weight" of a person by about 90 percent, which means that the stress on joints, bones, and muscles is similarly reduced. For this reason, it is unlikely that a water workout will result in injury or leave you with sore muscles. That's why the pool is such a great place for kids who are new to exercise or kids who are overweight. It is also a great form of exercise for families to share together because it challenges everyone from a beginner level to a toned athlete. For more exercises you can do in the pool, check out another one of my books, *101 Cool Pool Games for Children*, by Kim Rodomista.

Treading Intervals

Tell the children: Tread water as hard as you can for 30 seconds and then float on your back for 30 seconds. Repeat this sequence 30 times.

Water Sprints

Tell the children: In the pool, you can run in the shallow or deep end or do a combination of both. To increase speed and power in your run, try the following workout in the pool.

- Jog: Jog 3 to 5 minutes at a medium pace.
- Speed: Perform six 2-minute runs at a full run; jog for 60 seconds in between each 2-minute run.
- Sprint 1: Perform ten 60-second runs at medium speed; in between the sets, run as fast as you can for 30 seconds.
- Sprint 2: Run as fast as you can in the water for 10 seconds, keeping your arms under the water. Slow to a jog for 10 seconds and then repeat the sequence.
- Backward: Repeat the entire sequence above but run backward.

Water Push-Ups

Tell the children: Stand in a pool facing the pool stairs. Move your upper body forward until your hands rest on the top step of the pool steps. Go into a Plank Position (#41), with your arms straightened below your shoulders, your body forming a straight line from your head to your feet, and your feet touching the pool bottom. Keeping your spine straight, slowly lower your body as low as you can by bending at the elbows. Slowly push your body back up into the plank position, using your arms, and repeat. Do as many of these as you can until you can't do another repetition successfully and with control.

Kickboard Exercises

Using a kickboard or a noodle in both hands, try the following exercises:

- swim with legs alternating kick
- kick with one leg only and then switch legs
- frog legs
- sidestroke
- backstroke
- flutter kick

Alphabetical List of Games

The Games Arranged by Specific Categories

Games Requiring a Large Space

Games in Which Physical Contact Might Be Involved

Games Requiring an Exercise Mat

Games Requiring Props

●●● | ●●● | ●●● | ●●● | ●●● | ●●● | ●●● | ●●● | ●●● | ●●● | ●●● | ●●● | ●●● | ●●● | ●●● | ●●●